TEST IT FIX IT

PRE-INTERMEDIATE

DON'T JUST TEST IT, FIX IT!

English Grammar

Kenna Bourke

OXFORD
UNIVERSITY PRESS

Great Clarendon Street, Oxford OX2 6DP

Oxford University Press is a department of the University of Oxford. It furthers the University's objective of excellence in research, scholarship, and education by publishing worldwide in

Oxford New York

Auckland Bangkok Buenos Aires Cape Town Chennai Dar es Salaam Delhi Hong Kong Istanbul Karachi Kolkata Kuala Lumpur Madrid Melbourne Mexico City Mumbai Nairobi São Paulo Shanghai Taipei Tokyo Toronto

First published 2003

ISBN 0 19 4386201

Illustrated by Ken Pyne

Printed in China

Contents

How to use *Test it, Fix it*

Test it, Fix it is a series of books designed to help you identify any problems you may have in English, and to fix the problems. Each *Test it, Fix it* book has twenty tests which concentrate on mistakes commonly made by learners.

Test it, Fix it has an unusual format. You start at the **first** page of each unit, then go to the **third** page, then to the **second** page. Here's how it works:

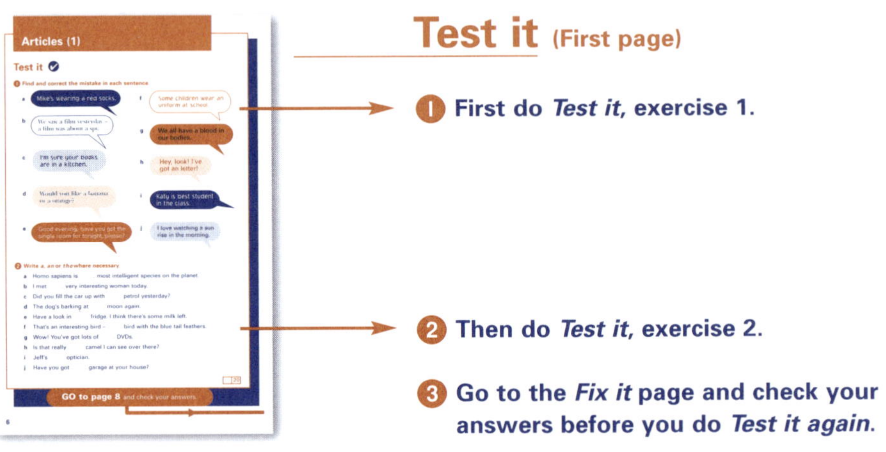

Test it (First page)

1 First do *Test it*, exercise 1.

2 Then do *Test it*, exercise 2.

3 Go to the *Fix it* page and check your answers before you do *Test it again*.

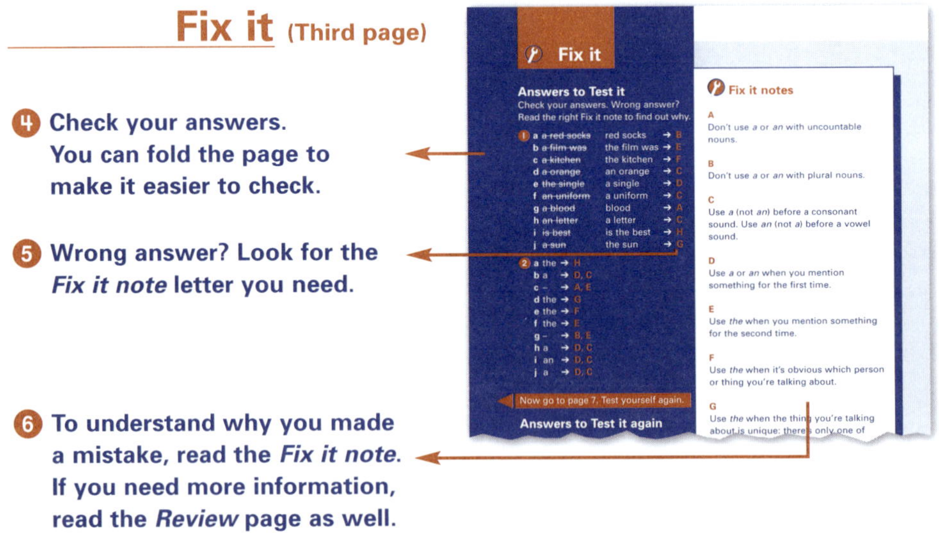

Fix it (Third page)

4 Check your answers. You can fold the page to make it easier to check.

5 Wrong answer? Look for the *Fix it note* letter you need.

6 To understand why you made a mistake, read the *Fix it note*. If you need more information, read the *Review* page as well.

7 Now go back to the second page and do *Test it again*.

Test it again (Second page)

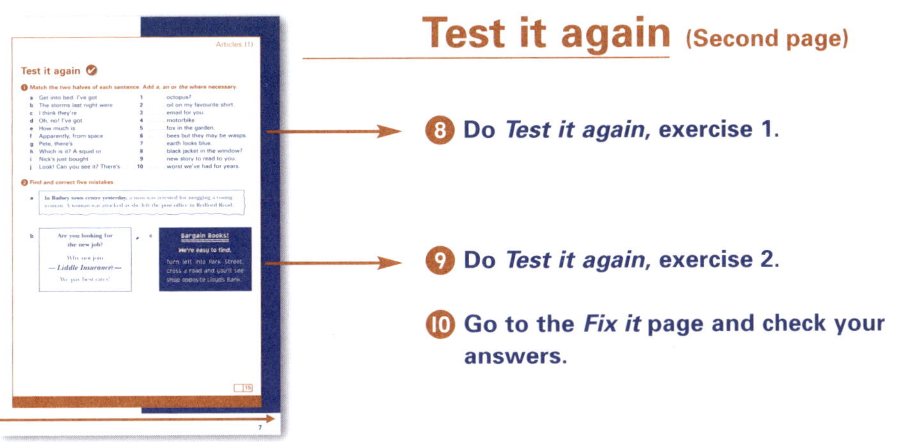

❽ Do *Test it again*, exercise 1.

❾ Do *Test it again*, exercise 2.

❿ Go to the *Fix it* page and check your answers.

Fix it (Third page)

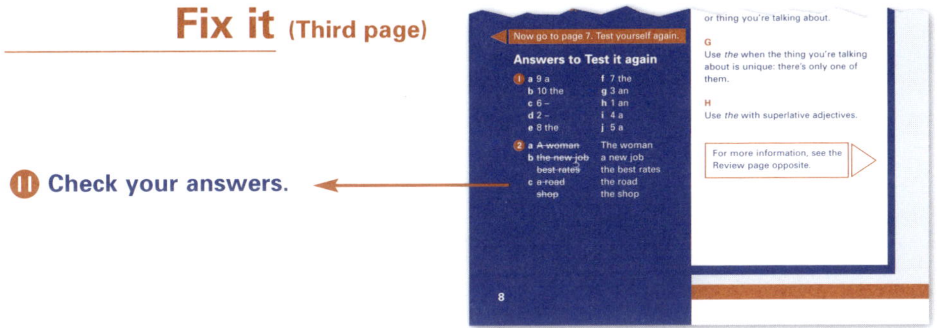

⓫ Check your answers.

Review (Fourth page)

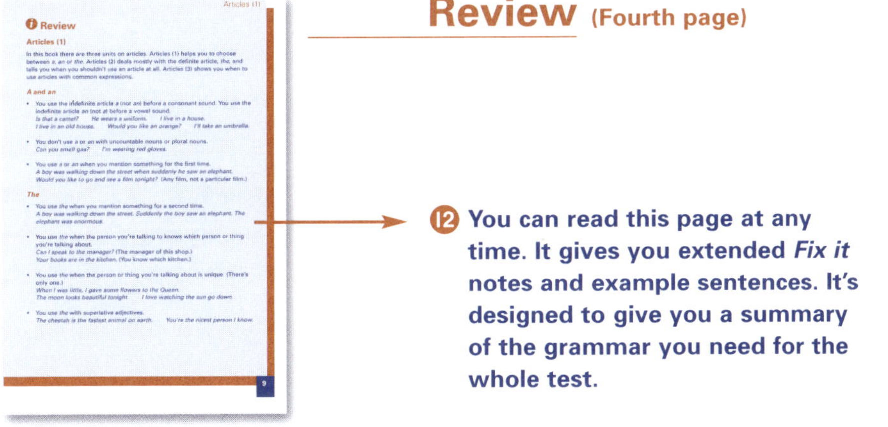

⓬ You can read this page at any time. It gives you extended *Fix it* notes and example sentences. It's designed to give you a summary of the grammar you need for the whole test.

Articles (1)

Test it ✔

1 Find and correct the mistake in each sentence.

a Mike's wearing a red socks.

b We saw a film yesterday – a film was about a spy.

c I'm sure your books are in a kitchen.

d Would you like a banana or a orange?

e Good evening, have you got the single room for tonight, please?

f Some children wear an uniform at school.

g We all have a blood in our bodies.

h Hey, look! I've got an letter!

i Katy is best student in the class.

j I love watching a sun rise in the morning.

2 Write *a, an* or *the* where necessary.

a Homo sapiens is .... most intelligent species on the planet.

b I met .... very interesting woman today.

c Did you fill the car up with .... petrol yesterday?

d The dog's barking at .... moon again.

e Have a look in .... fridge. I think there's some milk left.

f That's an interesting bird – .... bird with the blue tail feathers.

g Wow! You've got lots of .... DVDs.

h Is that really .... camel I can see over there?

i Jeff's .... optician.

j Have you got .... garage at your house?

[ ] 20

GO to page 8 and check your answers.

Test it again ✓

1 Match the two halves of each sentence. Add *a, an* or *the* where necessary.

a	Get into bed. I've got	**1**	.... octopus?
b	The storms last night were	**2**	.... oil on my favourite shirt.
c	I think they're	**3**	.... email for you.
d	Oh, no! I've got	**4**	.... motorbike.
e	How much is	**5**	.... fox in the garden.
f	Apparently, from space	**6**	.... bees but they may be wasps.
g	Pete, there's	**7**	.... earth looks blue.
h	Which is it? A squid or	**8**	.... black jacket in the window?
i	Nick's just bought	**9**	.... new story to read to you.
j	Look! Can you see it? There's	**10**	.... worst we've had for years.

2 Find and correct five mistakes.

a **In Badsey town centre yesterday,** a man was arrested for mugging a young woman. A woman was attacked as she left the post office in Redford Road.

b **Are you looking for the new job?**

Why not join

— ***Liddle Insurance*?** —

We pay best rates!

c **Bargain Books!**

We're easy to find.

Turn left into Park Street, cross a road and you'll see shop opposite Lloyds Bank.

15

Fix it

Answers to Test it

Check your answers. Wrong answer? Read the right Fix it note to find out why.

1
- **a** ~~a red socks~~ red socks → B
- **b** ~~a film was~~ the film was → E
- **c** ~~a kitchen~~ the kitchen → F
- **d** ~~a orange~~ an orange → C
- **e** ~~the single~~ a single → D
- **f** ~~an uniform~~ a uniform → C
- **g** ~~a blood~~ blood → A
- **h** ~~an letter~~ a letter → C
- **i** ~~is best~~ is the best → H
- **j** ~~a sun~~ the sun → G

2
- **a** the → H
- **b** a → D, C
- **c** – → A, E
- **d** the → G
- **e** the → F
- **f** the → E
- **g** – → B, E
- **h** a → D, C
- **i** an → D, C
- **j** a → D, C

Now go to page 7. Test yourself again.

Answers to Test it again

1
- **a** 9 a
- **b** 10 the
- **c** 6 –
- **d** 2 –
- **e** 8 the
- **f** 7 the
- **g** 3 an
- **h** 1 an
- **i** 4 a
- **j** 5 a

2
- **a** ~~A woman~~ The woman
- **b** ~~the new job~~ a new job
  ~~best rates~~ the best rates
- **c** ~~a road~~ the road
  ~~shop~~ the shop

Fix it notes

A

Don't use *a* or *an* with uncountable nouns.

B

Don't use *a* or *an* with plural nouns.

C

Use *a* (not *an*) before a consonant sound. Use *an* (not *a*) before a vowel sound.

D

Use *a* or *an* when you mention something for the first time.

E

Use *the* when you mention something for the second time.

F

Use *the* when it's obvious which person or thing you're talking about.

G

Use *the* when the thing you're talking about is unique: there's only one of them.

H

Use *the* with superlative adjectives.

For more information, see the Review page opposite.

Articles (1)

In this book there are three units on articles. Articles (1) helps you to choose between *a*, *an* or *the*. Articles (2) deals mostly with the definite article, *the*, and tells you when you shouldn't use an article at all. Articles (3) shows you when to use articles with common expressions.

A and *an*

- You use the indefinite article *a* (not *an*) before a consonant sound. You use the indefinite article *an* (not *a*) before a vowel sound.
  Is that a camel? *He wears a uniform.* *I live in a house.*
  I live in an old house. *Would you like an orange?* *I'll take an umbrella.*

- You don't use *a* or *an* with uncountable nouns or plural nouns.
  Can you smell gas? *I'm wearing red gloves.*

- You use *a* or *an* when you mention something for the first time.
  A boy was walking down the street when suddenly he saw an elephant.
  Would you like to go and see a film tonight? (Any film, not a particular film.)

The

- You use *the* when you mention something for a second time.
  A boy was walking down the street. Suddenly the boy saw an elephant. The elephant was enormous.

- You use *the* when the person you're talking to knows which person or thing you're talking about.
  Can I speak to the manager? (The manager of this shop.)
  Your books are in the kitchen. (You know which kitchen.)

- You use *the* when the person or thing you're talking about is unique. (There's only one.)
  When I was little, I gave some flowers to the Queen.
  The moon looks beautiful tonight. *I love watching the sun go down.*

- You use *the* with superlative adjectives.
  The cheetah is the fastest animal on earth. *You're the nicest person I know.*

Articles (2)

Test it ✔

1 Choose the best option, A or B.

- **a** I'm ....
  A a teacher **B** teacher
- **b** Could you open ....? I'm hot.
  A the window **B** window
- **c** Jeff wants to climb ....
  A the Mount Everest **B** Mount Everest
- **d** Do you enjoy listening to ....?
  A music **B** the music
- **e** I spent my childhood in ....
  A the Belgium **B** Belgium
- **f** We're going skiing in ....
  A Alps **B** the Alps
- **g** Jack's got ....
  A the loud voice **B** a loud voice
- **h** My doctor says .... is bad for you.
  A salt **B** the salt
- **i** Can you pass me ...., please?
  A salt **B** the salt
- **j** My brother speaks ....
  A the French **B** French

2 Choose the best option.

- **a** The Dr Smith/Dr Smith was a lecturer at London University.
- **b** Tom van Vuren comes from the Netherlands/Netherlands.
- **c** The clown had big red nose/a big red nose.
- **d** I've always loved Italian/the Italian. It's such a musical language.
- **e** Stephen, the children/children are ready to go to school.
- **f** Do you eat the chicken/chicken or are you vegetarian?
- **g** Have you ever been to Lake Orta/the Lake Orta? It's very beautiful.
- **h** We're staying at Sheraton Hotel/the Sheraton Hotel tonight.
- **i** Nicholas is an architect/architect, isn't he?
- **j** I think the Lia/Lia is a very pretty baby.

	20

GO to page 12 and check your answers.

Test it again ✓

1 Complete the sentences. Use *a, an* or *the* where necessary.

- **a** You really have got .... lovely smile!
- **b** Sarah wants to sail on .... Nile.
- **c** I'm spending New Year's Eve in .... Brussels.
- **d** Can you pass me .... water?
- **e** All living creatures need .... water.
- **f** I don't like .... fish. Too many bones!
- **g** Mireia comes from .... Spain, doesn't she?
- **h** .... Chinese is a difficult language to learn.
- **i** Joe wants to be .... airline pilot.
- **j** .... Taj Mahal is an amazing building.

2 Find and correct twelve mistakes in these dialogues.

a Tim: Dan, do you want sugar in your coffee?
Dan: Yes, please. I know the sugar's bad for your teeth but I hate the coffee without it. The Dr Rawstorne tells me to give it up every time I see him.

b Carol: Wow! This guidebook is great. Have you ever been up Eiffel Tower?
Nick: No, in fact I've never been to the France. Pass me guidebook, please.

c Harry: The dictionaries are so expensive these days!
Sally: Yes, I know, but books cost a lot to make, don't they?

d Pete: I've decided I don't want to be politician after all.
Jill: Good. I don't like the politicians anyway.

e Victor: The David is going to United States soon to study economics.
Sarah: Oh, yes, I remember. He's going to the New York, isn't he?

	22

Fix it

Answers to Test it

Check your answers. Wrong answer? Read the right Fix it note to find out why.

1
- **a** A → A
- **b** A → B
- **c** B → D
- **d** A → C
- **e** B → D
- **f** B → E
- **g** B → A
- **h** A → C
- **i** B → B
- **j** B → D

2
- **a** Dr Smith → D
- **b** the Netherlands → E
- **c** a big red nose → A
- **d** Italian → D
- **e** the children → B
- **f** chicken → C
- **g** Lake Orta → D
- **h** the Sheraton Hotel → E
- **i** an architect → A
- **j** Lia → D

Now go to page 11. Test yourself again.

Answers to Test it again

1
- **a** a
- **b** the
- **c** –
- **d** the
- **e** –
- **f** –
- **g** –
- **h** –
- **i** an
- **j** The

2

a	~~the sugar's~~	sugar's
	~~the coffee~~	coffee
	~~The Doctor~~	Doctor
b	~~Eiffel Tower~~	the Eiffel Tower
	~~the France~~	France
	~~guidebook~~	the guidebook
c	~~The dictionaries~~	Dictionaries
d	~~politician~~	a politician
	~~the politicians~~	politicians
e	~~The David~~	David
	~~United States~~	the United States
	~~the New York~~	New York

Fix it notes

A

Use *a* or *an* before a noun or before an adjective + noun to describe something or to say what someone's job is.

B

Use *the* when the person you're talking to knows which person or thing you're talking about.

C

Don't use an article when you're talking about things in a general way, e.g. *chicken, music, salt*.

D

Don't use an article to talk about a person, a language or most places, including the name of a country, a mountain or a lake.

E

Use *the* with the names of places that are plural; the names of deserts, seas, rivers and oceans; and the names of most buildings.

For more information, see the Review page opposite.

Review

Articles (2)

A and *an*

- You use *a* or *an* to describe things and to say what someone's job is.
  This is a good book. *Helen is an editor.* NOT ~~*Helen is editor.*~~

The

- You use *the* when the person you're talking to knows which person or thing you're talking about.
  Could you pass me the salt? (The salt that's on the table.)
  Your glasses are in the car. (It's our car. You know which one I mean.)

- You use *the* with the names of places that are plural, e.g. *the United States, the Netherlands; the United Arab Emirates.* You also use *the* with the names of most deserts, seas, rivers and oceans, and with the names of most buildings.
  Robin lives in the United States. *She sailed across the Pacific.*
  It's very hot in the Negev Desert. *I found the book in the British Library.*

  Note, however, that there are exceptions to this rule. You don't use *the* with the names of buildings which include the words *school, university, college; castle, palace; airport, station,* e.g. *London University, Topkapi Palace; Frankfurt Airport.*

No article

- You don't use an article (*a, an* or *the*) when you're talking about things in general. If you use an article, you change the meaning.
  I like milk but I don't like fish. (All milk and all fish.)
  Please pass me the milk. (The milk that's on the table.)
  Children are adorable. (All children.)
  The children are adorable. (Our children.)

- You don't use an article with languages or with the names of most places.
  Paddy speaks French. NOT ~~*Paddy speaks the French.*~~
  We like Lake Como. NOT ~~*We like the Lake Como.*~~

  Note, however, that there are exceptions to this rule. You use *the* with the names of places which include words such as *kingdom, sultanate, republic,* e.g. *The Republic of Ireland,* and with very big parts of the world, e.g. *The Far East.*

- You don't use an article before people's names or before *Mr, Ms, Mrs, Miss, Dr, Professor,* etc. and the person's name.
  Tony is my best friend. NOT ~~*The Tony is my best friend.*~~
  Dr Rawstorne is nice. NOT ~~*The Dr Rawstorne is nice.*~~
  Mrs Baum teaches history. NOT ~~*The Mrs Baum teaches history.*~~

Articles (3)

Test it ✓

1 Choose the correct sentence in each pair.

a John's in the hospital because he's broken his leg.
b John's in hospital because he's broken his leg.

c What funny boy you are!
d What a funny boy you are!

e We'll have a salad for lunch.
f We'll have a salad for the lunch.

g We're going to London by the car.
h We're going to London by car.

i To get to Broad Street, take the second turning on the left.
j To get to Broad Street, take the second turning on left.

2 Write *a*, *an* or *the* where necessary.

a Mickey James is in .... prison again.

b Hey, look! My watch is .... same as yours!

c Emma's only five and she can already count to .... hundred.

d The children go to school by .... bus.

e Would you like to win .... million dollars?

f Julian! What .... amazing surprise!

g What do you want for .... breakfast?

h Patrick Leigh Fermor travelled from London to Istanbul on .... foot.

i Sandy's working as .... assistant until she goes to Australia.

j Take the third turning on .... right.

☐ 15

GO to page 16 and check your answers.

Test it again

1 Find and correct the mistake in each sentence.

a David always uses his pen as spoon.

b I counted thousand coins in fifteen minutes!

c Do you want to have the dinner with me?

d You and me – we're same type of people.

e What lovely house!

f I hate travelling by the plane.

g Why don't you ring Fiona? I think she's at the home.

h The kids love going to cinema.

i I can't see you on Saturday because I'm going to the work.

j You turn the lights off! I don't want to get out of the bed.

2 Match the two halves of each sentence. Add *a, an* or *the* where necessary.

a	Do you ever go to	**1**	.... helicopter.
b	The post office is over there on	**2**	.... waiter at the moment.
c	We often go to the beach in	**3**	.... hospital.
d	Most people dislike being in	**4**	.... church?
e	I'm busy. I've got	**5**	.... June.
f	Harry! What	**6**	.... lunch we'll play football.
g	He's working as	**7**	.... coast more than the mountains.
h	They do mountain rescues by	**8**	.... million things to do.
i	After	**9**	.... surprise to see you again!
j	I like	**10**	.... right next to the bank.

    /20

Fix it

Answers to Test it

Check your answers. Wrong answer? Read the right Fix it note to find out why.

1 The correct sentences are:

b → B h → E
d → F i → A
e → C

2
a – → B
b the → A
c a → G
d – → E
e a → G
f an → F
g – → C
h – → E
i an → D
j the → A

Now go to page 15. Test yourself again.

Answers to Test it again

1
a ~~spoon~~ a spoon
b ~~thousand~~ a thousand
c ~~the dinner~~ dinner
d ~~same~~ the same
e ~~lovely~~ a lovely
f ~~by the plane~~ by plane
g ~~the home~~ home
h ~~cinema~~ the cinema
i ~~the work~~ work
j ~~the bed~~ bed

2
a 4 – f 9 a
b 10 the g 2 a
c 5 – h 1 –
d 3 – i 6 –
e 8 a j 7 the

Fix it notes

A
Use *the* before some common expressions, e.g. *the left, the right, the same.*

B
Don't use an article with some common expressions relating to particular places, e.g. *in bed, at home, in hospital, in prison, to work.*

C
Don't use an article with meals, days, months, or with holidays, festivals and special days.

D
Use *a* or *an* before a singular countable noun after *as.*

E
Don't use an article with methods of transport, e.g. *by bus, by car, on foot.*

F
Use *a* or *an* before a singular countable noun in exclamations with *What ... !*

G
Use *a* before *hundred, thousand, million* when you mean 'one hundred', 'one thousand', etc.

For more information, see the Review page opposite.

Review

Articles (3)

A and *an*

- You use *a* or *an* before singular countable nouns after *as*.
  I'm using my spare bedroom as an office.
  Jane's working as an assistant in the doctor's surgery. NOT ~~*as assistant*~~

- You use *a* or *an* before singular countable nouns in exclamations that start with *What.*
  What a surprise! *What an amazing car!* *What a funny dream!*

- You use *a* before the words *hundred, thousand, million, billion,* etc. when you mean 'one hundred', 'one thousand', etc.
  Jill's won a hundred euros. *A thousand years ago there was a forest here.*

The

- You use *the* before some common expressions, e.g. *the same, the cinema, the theatre, the right, the left, the top, the coast,* etc. You need to learn these.
  You're wearing the same jacket as me. *Shall we go to the cinema?*
  My house is on the left.

No article

- You don't use an article with some common expressions relating to particular places.
  to, in or *out of:* bed, church, hospital, prison
  to, at or *from*: college, school, university, work

  Bob will be in prison for six months. NOT ~~in the prison~~
  We learnt a lot at school today. NOT ~~at the school~~
  I like going to work. NOT ~~the work~~

- You don't use an article with meals, days, months, holidays, festivals and special days.
  Let's have lunch together. *I hate Mondays.* *My birthday's in June.*
  The kids love Christmas. *We always have a party on New Year's Day.*

- You don't use an article with methods of transport.
  I get to work by train. *Helen loves going everywhere on foot.*
  It's quicker by car. *The Prime Minister travels by plane.*

Adjectives and adverbs

Test it ✔

1 Five of these sentences are incorrect. Find and correct them.

a Steve hit the ball hard.

b You're a person nice.

c Harry is a dog black.

d *The Economist* is a weekly magazine.

e This curry tastes wonderful.

f Rabbit fur feels softly.

g We saw two beautifuls sunsets last week.

h Did you get up very early?

i Buy some green apples.

j I bought today a car.

2 Choose the correct sentence in each pair.

a Malcolm speaks well Italian.
b Malcolm speaks Italian well.

c That perfume smells wonderful!
d That perfume smells wonderfully!

e A kitten is a cat young.
f A kitten is a young cat.

g They test weekly the fire alarms.
h They test the fire alarms weekly.

i I read five good books on holiday.
j I read five goods books on holiday.

☐ 15

GO to page 20 and check your answers.

Test it again ✓

1 Solve the clues to complete the crossword. Use the words below.

bad badly easy easily good well
slow slowly soft softly strange strangely

Across

2 The hairdresser cut my hair .... yesterday.
3 The soup tastes .... What's in it?
5 Our French exam was quite ....
7 Have you seen any .... films recently?
8 My rabbit has .... white fur.
9 Danger. Drive ....
11 Nick is a .... reader but he loves books.

Down

1 You're talking .... Have you got toothache?
4 The meat smells .... Let's throw it away.
5 I can .... drink three litres of water a day.
6 'Don't worry,' she said ....
10 Thierry Hervé played really .... in the match.

2 Choose the best option.

a Patrick has hair blond/blond hair.
b Sue didn't enjoy much the film/the film much.
c You look angry/angrily – what's wrong?
d Vicky shouted loudly/loud.
e The Alps are very snowys/snowy in winter.
f The music sounds cheerful/cheerfully.
g The situation is serious/seriously.
h Don't drive so fast/fastly.
i *The Times* is a paper daily/daily paper.
j This tastes delicious/deliciously!

☐ 22

Fix it

Answers to Test it

Check your answers. Wrong answer?
Read the right Fix it note to find out why.

1
- **a** correct → D
- **b** ~~person nice~~ nice person → A
- **c** ~~dog black~~ black dog → A
- **d** correct → E
- **e** correct → C
- **f** ~~softly~~ soft → C
- **g** ~~beautifuls~~ beautiful → B
- **h** correct → E
- **i** correct → B
- **j** ~~today a car~~ a car today → D

2 The correct sentences are:
- **b** → D
- **c** → C
- **f** → A
- **h** → D
- **i** → B

Now go to page 19. Test yourself again.

Answers to Test it again

1

2
- **a** blond hair
- **b** the film much
- **c** angry
- **d** loudly
- **e** snowy
- **f** cheerful
- **g** serious
- **h** fast
- **i** daily paper
- **j** delicious

Fix it notes

A

Put adjectives before (not after) nouns or pronouns.

B

Adjectives don't change their form with singular or plural nouns.

C

Put adjectives (not adverbs) after these verbs: *appear, be, become, feel, get, look, seem, smell, sound, taste.*

D

Don't put adverbs between the verb and the object. Usually put them at the end of the sentence.

E

Early and *late; fast* and *hard; daily, weekly* and *monthly* are adjectives and adverbs.

For more information, see the Review page opposite.

Review

Adjectives and adverbs

Adjectives

- You use adjectives to say more about a noun or a pronoun. Adjectives go before (not after) the noun or pronoun.
  He's a man. *He's a nice man.* NOT ~~*He's a man nice.*~~
  Harry's a dog. *Harry's a black dog.* NOT ~~*Harry is a dog black.*~~

- You don't change the form of an adjective with singular or plural nouns.
  It's an interesting book. *These are interesting books.* NOT ~~*interestings*~~
  Those shoes are cheap. NOT ~~*cheaps*~~

- You put adjectives after (not before) these verbs: *appear, be, become, feel, get, look, seem, smell, sound, taste.*
  You look tired. NOT ~~*You tired look.*~~
  That seems easy. NOT ~~*That easy seems.*~~

- You use an adjective (not an adverb) after these verbs: *appear, be, become, feel, get, look, seem, smell, sound, taste.*
  The bread smells wonderful. NOT ~~*wonderfully*~~
  Does the milk taste bad? NOT ~~*badly*~~

Adverbs

- You form most adverbs by adding *ly* to the adjective.
  quick ➔ *quickly*
  But be careful. Some adverbs are irregular.
  good ➔ *well* *She's a good runner.* *She runs well.*
  hard ➔ *hard* *Digging is hard work.* *He works hard.*

- You use adverbs to say more about verbs. Adverbs tell you how, where, when or how much something happens. You usually put them at the end of the sentence. You don't put them between the verb and its object.
  They sell delicious pizzas here. NOT ~~*They sell here delicious pizzas.*~~
  You speak French well. NOT ~~*You speak well French.*~~

Adjectives and adverbs

- *Early* and *late; hard* and *fast; daily, weekly* and *monthly* can be adjectives and adverbs.
  He always catches the early train. *I got up early.*
  I always get a daily paper. *They publish* The Times *daily.*

Word order with adjectives

Test it ✔

1 Find and correct any sentences that are wrong.

a I saw a white little mouse in the kitchen.

b Katy lives in a small modern flat near the town centre.

c Venice is an old beautiful city.

d Yuck! This horrible tastes!

e Jim gave me a grey cotton scarf.

f Nicky is small, fair and blue-eyed.

g It was the third big surprise of the day.

h Please buy me large two bottles of milk.

i The important is that I love you.

j It was a journey tiring.

2 Choose the correct sentence in each pair.

a You tired look.
b You look tired.

c You need large two eggs.
d You need two large eggs.

e An Italian leather handbag.
f A leather Italian handbag.

g The poor boy is ill.
h The poor is ill.

i She drives a tiny white car.
j She drives a white tiny car.

k What a nice little boy!
l What a little nice boy!

m It good tastes!
n It tastes good!

o They're football black boots.
p They're black football boots.

q He's tall, thin and blond.
r He's tall, thin, blond.

s He's got five Siamese cats.
t He's got Siamese five cats.

☐ 20

GO to page 24 and check your answers.

Test it again ✔

1 Put the adjectives in the correct order before the nouns.

a	Nepalese/red/beautiful	scarf
b	tall/thin/blue-eyed	man
c	big/first	match
d	cycling/blue/lycra	shorts
e	Belgian/hot/delicious	chips
f	ballet/silk/pink	shoes
g	scary/French	film
h	German/shepherd/dangerous	dog
i	long/fifth	email
j	yellow/seven/tiny	ducks

2 Choose the correct option, A or B.

a I bought .... music box.
A a lovely Italian **B** an Italian lovely

b Jo's got a .... car.
A black huge sports **B** huge black sports

c That's the .... thing you've said!
A stupid third **B** third stupid

d I live in .... house.
A an old stone **B** a stone old

e That was .... curry!
A a spicy excellent **B** an excellent spicy

f You ....
A seem unhappy **B** unhappy seem

g Could you pass me the .... ruler?
A metal long **B** long metal

h The room looks ....
A light sunny **B** light and sunny

i We need a .... dictionary.
A good French **B** French good

j Smuff is .... rabbit.
A an adorable little Dutch **B** a Dutch little adorable

[ ] 20

Fix it

Answers to Test it

Check your answers. Wrong answer? Read the right Fix it note to find out why.

1
- a ~~white little~~ little white → A
- b correct → A
- c ~~an old beautiful~~ a beautiful old → C
- d ~~horrible tastes~~ tastes horrible → F
- e correct → B
- f correct → A, G
- g correct → D
- h ~~large two~~ two large → D
- i ~~important is~~ important thing is → E
- j ~~journey tiring~~ tiring journey → E

2 The correct sentences are:

b → F	k → C
d → D	n → F
e → B	p → B
g → E	q → G
i → A	s → D

Now go to page 23. Test yourself again.

Answers to Test it again

1
- a beautiful red Nepalese
- b tall thin blue-eyed
- c first big
- d blue lycra cycling
- e delicious hot Belgian
- f pink silk ballet
- g scary French
- h dangerous German shepherd
- i fifth long
- j seven tiny yellow

2

a A	b B	c B	d A	e B
f A	g B	h B	i A	j A

Fix it notes

A
Put adjectives describing size, length or height before other adjectives but after adjectives describing opinion.

B
Put adjectives describing colour, origin, material and purpose in that order.

C
Put adjectives describing opinion, e.g. *beautiful*, before any other adjectives.

D
Put numbers before adjectives.

E
Adjectives go before (not after) a noun. Always put a noun, e.g. *thing, boy*, after an adjective except in special cases.

F
Put adjectives after (not before) these verbs: *appear, be, become, feel, get, look, seem, smell, sound* and *taste*.

G
Use *and* before the last adjective if you use two or more adjectives after *appear, be, become, feel, get, look, seem, smell, sound* and *taste*.

For more information, see the Review page opposite.

Review

Word order with adjectives

It's impossible to give exact rules for word order with adjectives in English because there are many exceptions. However, there are some guidelines that will help you to choose the correct word order in most cases. Generally you don't use more than three adjectives together in the same sentence.

- You usually put adjectives that describe your opinion before any other adjectives.
  John's handsome, slim and fair-haired. *What an adorable little baby!*

- You use adjectives that describe size, length or height before adjectives that describe colour, origin, material or purpose.
  He's got a big red nose. *That's a small Dutch rabbit.* *It's a long silk scarf.*
  He drives a black racing car.

- You use adjectives that describe colour, origin, material or purpose in that order.
  These are green Alsatian glass drinking cups.
  Bill is a brown German shepherd dog.

- You put numbers and words like *first, second, last,* etc. before adjectives.
  Three ripe tomatoes. *That's the last boring party I'm going to.*

- Adjectives go before (not after) a noun. Don't use an adjective on its own.
  It's a long walk. NOT ~~*It's a walk long.*~~
  The important thing is that we love each other. NOT ~~*The important is that ...*~~
  The poor girl is unwell. NOT ~~*The poor is unwell.*~~

  Note: You can use an adjective without a noun in special cases, e.g. *the elderly, the poor, the unemployed, the young,* etc. In these cases, you're talking about a group of people and you're using the adjective as a noun.
  This charity raises money for the poor. (Poor people as a group.)

- Put adjectives after (not before) these verbs: *appear, be, become, feel, get, look, seem, sound, smell* and *taste*.
  You look beautiful! *He seems happy.* *I feel tired.* NOT ~~*I tired feel.*~~

- After *appear, be, become, feel, get, look, seem, sound, smell* and *taste*, you use *and* before the last adjective if you use two or more adjectives in the same sentence. If you use three adjectives, you put a comma after the first adjective.
  It tastes nice and spicy. *You look tired and unhappy.*
  The article was interesting, amusing and well-written.
  He was thin, old and homeless.

Word order with adverbs

Test it ✔

1 Choose the correct sentence in each pair.

a He often forgets to ring me.
b He forgets often to ring me.

c She didn't like much the film.
d She didn't like the film much.

e The report is finished completely.
f The report is completely finished.

g I speak Italian badly.
h I speak badly Italian.

i Did you see Martina yesterday?
j Did you yesterday see Martina?

k I feel sad very.
l I feel very sad.

m We always have lived here.
n We have always lived here.

o They make here wonderful sandwiches.
p They make wonderful sandwiches here.

q Have you studied always at this school?
r Have you always studied at this school?

s I'll probably see you on Friday.
t I'll see you probably on Friday.

2 Put the adverbs in the correct places.

a Pete and Sue are married. (happily)
b David gets up early. (always)
c Have you got your dog? (still)
d I enjoyed the film. (a lot)
e We're leaving. (today)
f He feels ill. (terribly)
g You left your book. (there)
h Tom plays the drums. (well)
i I'll ring you tomorrow. (definitely)
j Tony knows the answer. (probably)

| | 20 |

GO to page 28 and check your answers.

Test it again ✓

1 Five of these sentences are incorrect. Find and correct them.

a Do you go to the theatre ever?

b Keith doesn't often come round.

c Will I see you tomorrow?

d The cake is overcooked totally.

e We sometimes go out to a restaurant.

f Simon can help you probably.

g They sell here postcards.

h I never want to do this again.

i Are you usually cheerful?

j She doesn't very well ride a bike.

2 Choose the best option, A or B.

a Do you .... me?
A still love **B** love still

b Fiona doesn't have a sense of humour. She ....
A laughs never **B** never laughs

c Finish your homework quickly. Supper is ....
A almost ready **B** ready almost

d No one enjoyed ....
A much the play **B** the play much

e We watch ....
A TV a lot **B** a lot TV

f How long have you ....?
A there lived **B** lived there

g Rabbits ....
A run fast **B** fast run

h You look ....
A extremely happy **B** happy extremely

i Let's ....
A tomorrow go out **B** go out tomorrow

j He sings ....
A very loudly **B** loudly very

[ ] /20

Fix it

Answers to Test it

Check your answers. Wrong answer? Read the right Fix it note to find out why.

1 The correct sentences are:

a → A **l** → H
d → D **n** → B
f → H **p** → E
g → G **r** → C
i → F **s** → B

2
a are happily married → H
b always gets up early → A
c Have you still got → C
d the film a lot → D
e We're leaving today. → F
f He feels terribly ill. → H
g left your book there → E
h plays the drums well → G
i I'll definitely ring → B
j Tony probably knows → A

Now go to page 27. Test yourself again.

Answers to Test it again

1
a ~~Do you go ... ever?~~
Do you ever go ...?
b correct
c correct
d ~~overcooked totally.~~
totally overcooked.
e correct
f ~~help you probably.~~
probably help you.
g ~~here postcards.~~
postcards here.
h correct
i correct
j ~~very well ride a bike.~~
ride a bike very well.

2 **a** A **b** B **c** A **d** B **e** A
f B **g** A **h** A **i** B **j** A

Fix it notes

A
Put adverbs of frequency, e.g. *often*, and certainty, e.g. *probably*, before most verbs.

B
Put adverbs of frequency, e.g. *always*, and certainty, e.g. *definitely*, after auxiliary verbs and the verb *be*.

C
In questions, put adverbs of frequency, e.g. *always*, after auxiliary + subject.

D
Put adverbs of quantity, e.g. *much*, at the end of the sentence (not between the verb and its object).

E
Put adverbs of place, e.g. *here*, at the end of the sentence (not between the verb and its object).

F
Put adverbs of time, e.g. *yesterday*, at the end of the sentence (not between the verb and its object).

G
Put adverbs of manner, e.g. *badly*, at the end of the sentence (not between the verb and its object).

H
Put adverbs before (not after) an adjective or a past participle.

For more information, see the Review page opposite.

Review

Word order with adverbs

Different kinds of adverb, for example adverbs of frequency such as *always* or adverbs of manner such as *badly*, go in different positions in a sentence. Some go at the end of the sentence but others go near the verb.

Adverbs of frequency and certainty

- You use adverbs of frequency, e.g. *never, often, sometimes*, etc. and adverbs of certainty, e.g. *certainly, definitely, probably*, etc. before most verbs.
  We never go sailing. *I often go running.* *He definitely likes pizza.*

- You use adverbs of frequency and certainty after auxiliary verbs, e.g. *can, do, have, must, will*, etc. and after the verb *be*.
  I can often beat him at chess. *She has probably been there before.*

- In questions, you use adverbs of frequency and adverbs like *still* and *ever* after an auxiliary + subject.
  Do you often go out? *Does he still love me?* *Have you ever seen him?*

Adverbs of manner, place, quantity and time

- You usually use adverbs of manner, e.g. *badly, well*; adverbs of place, e.g. *here, there*; adverbs of quantity, e.g. *a bit, a lot, much;* and adverbs of time, e.g. *today, yesterday*, at the end of the sentence. Never put these adverbs between a verb and its object. This is a very common mistake.
  You speak English well. NOT ~~*You speak well English.*~~
  They sell stamps here. NOT ~~*They sell here stamps.*~~
  We liked the restaurant a lot. NOT ~~*We liked a lot the restaurant.*~~
  He's leaving the house today. NOT ~~*He's leaving today the house.*~~

Adverbs before adjectives and past participles

- You put adverbs before (not after) an adjective or a past participle.
  The book is nearly written. NOT ~~*The book is written nearly*~~.
  You look extremely tired. NOT ~~*You look tired extremely*~~.

Comparative and superlative adjectives

Test it ✔

1 Find and correct the mistake in each sentence.

a My brother is intelligenter than I am.

b The blue whale is the animal the biggest.

c Iceland is colder England.

d Nick is more kind than Alison.

e This is the most good film I've ever seen!

f Which skyscraper is the highest of the world?

g Mark finds Spanish easyer to learn than Italian.

h Today was the hotest day of the year.

i Isabelle is the more beautiful person I've met.

j These are ugliest shoes in the shop.

2 Write the comparative and superlative forms of these adjectives.

		comparative	superlative
a	nasty	....	....
b	nice	....	....
c	handsome	....	....
d	wet	....	....
e	far	....	....

☐ 15

GO to page 32 and check your answers.

Test it again ✓

1 Choose the best option, A or B.

a Are oysters .... than mussels?
A more tasty **B** tastier

b Skiing is .... exciting sport in the world.
A the most **B** a most

c That's the best painting .... the art gallery.
A in **B** of

d You're the .... person I know.
A funnier **B** funniest

e Is ancient Greek more difficult .... Latin?
A as **B** than

f Which is .... , Africa or Asia?
A hoter **B** hotter

g A cat can jump .... than a dog.
A higher **B** more high

h Michael is .... person to ask.
A best **B** the best

i She was much .... than I thought she would be.
A sillyer **B** sillier

j Who is .... ? Kate or Judith?
A fitter **B** more fitter

2 Find and correct five mistakes in the headlines.

a **Crows are more good toolmakers than chimpanzees.**

b **IT'S OFFICIAL:** *Beckham is best footballer of the world.*

c **Is this the discovery the greatest?**

d **Exclusive!** *The world's older man reaches 117th birthday.*

☐ 15

Fix it

Answers to Test it

Check your answers. Wrong answer? Read the right Fix it note to find out why.

1 **a** ~~intelligenter~~
more intelligent → B
b ~~the animal the biggest~~
the biggest animal → G
c ~~colder~~
colder than → F
d ~~more kind~~ kinder → A
e ~~most good~~ best → D
f ~~of the world~~
in the world → E
g ~~easyer~~ easier → B
h ~~hotest~~ hottest → C
i ~~more~~ most → B
j ~~ugliest~~ the ugliest → F

2 **a** nastier, the nastiest → B
b nicer, the nicest → A
c more handsome,
the most handsome → B
d wetter, the wettest → C
e further, the furthest → D

Now go to page 31. Test yourself again.

Answers to Test it again

1 **a** B **b** A **c** A **d** B **e** B
f B **g** A **h** B **i** B **j** A

2 **a** ~~more good~~ better
b ~~best~~ the best
~~of~~ in
c ~~the discovery the greatest~~
the greatest discovery
d ~~older~~ oldest

Fix it notes

A

Make the comparative and superlative of one-syllable adjectives ending in *e* by adding *r* and *st*. For other one-syllable adjectives add *er* and *est*.

B

Make the comparative and superlative of two-syllable adjectives ending in *y* by changing ~~*y*~~ to *i* and adding *er* and *est*. For other two syllable adjectives and longer adjectives, add *more* and *the most* before the adjective.

C

Double the last letter of adjectives that end in one vowel + one consonant, then add *er* and *est*.

D

Some adjectives have irregular comparative and superlative forms.

E

After a superlative use *in* (not *of*) with a singular word for a place or a group.

F

Use *than* after a comparative adjective and *the* before a superlative adjective.

G

Put comparative and superlative adjectives before the noun.

For more information, see the Review page opposite.

Comparative and superlative adjectives

- You make the comparative and superlative of one-syllable adjectives ending in *e* by adding *r* and *st*. You make the comparative and superlative of other one-syllable adjectives by adding *er* and *est*.
  nice nicer the nicest fast faster the fastest

- You need to double the last letter of adjectives that end in one vowel + one consonant, then add *er* and *est*.
  big bigger the biggest hot hotter the hottest
  fat fatter the fattest thin thinner the thinnest

- You make the comparative and superlative of two-syllable adjectives ending in *y* by changing *y* to *i* and adding *er* and *est*.
  easy easier the easiest tasty tastier the tastiest

- You make the comparative and superlative of other two-syllable adjectives and longer adjectives by adding *more* and *the most* before the adjective.
  boring more boring the most boring
  interesting more interesting the most interesting

- Some adjectives have an irregular comparative and superlative form. You need to learn these.
  good better the best far further the furthest
  bad worse the worst little less the least
  much/many more the most

- You use *than* after a comparative adjective and *the* before a superlative adjective.
  You're taller than me. John is the tallest in the class.

- You put the comparative or superlative adjective before (not after) the noun.
  The elephant is the biggest land animal. NOT ~~*... the land animal the biggest.*~~

Note: You don't use *of* with a singular word for a place or a group, e.g. *the world, the class, the team*. You use *in*. This is a very common mistake.
Is the cheetah the fastest animal in the world? NOT ~~*... of the world.*~~
Alice is the best student in the class. NOT ~~*... of the class.*~~

Comparative and superlative adverbs

Test it ✔

1 Complete the sentences. Use the comparative or superlative form of the adverbs in brackets.

- **a** Richard's clever, but Bob works .... of all the students. (hard)
- **b** They all danced well, but Ellen danced .... (elegantly)
- **c** Mary drives .... than Andrea. (badly)
- **d** You get high marks .... than I do. (often)
- **e** Could you come .... than ten? It's rather late. (early)

2 Find and correct ten mistakes on the webpage.

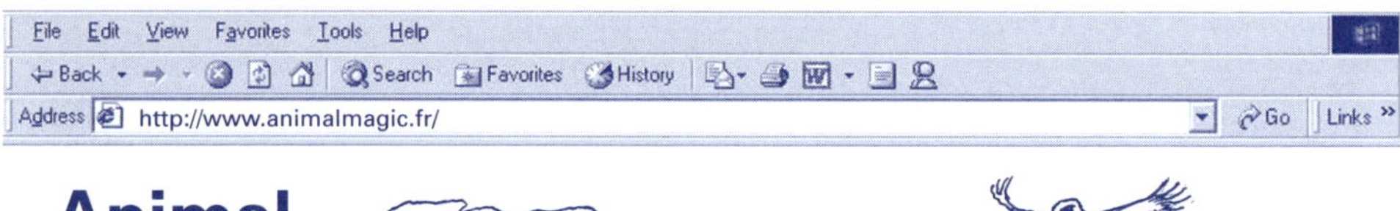

Animal FAQs

- **a** Can tortoises walk faster turtles?
- **b** Of all the birds in the world, which bird sings the best?
- **c** Do other animals wake up more early than birds or are birds the first to wake up?
- **d** Which animal eats more greedily – a lion, a tiger or a leopard?
- **e** Do worker bees really work harder than other bees?
- **f** Can chimpanzees climb trees easily than orang-utans?
- **g** Do camels live longer elephants?
- **h** Can bats see clearly than humans?
- **i** Which flies highest – an eagle or a hawk?
- **j** Why don't zookeepers get bitten oftener?
- **k** Do alligators move more slowly than crocodiles?
- **l** Can dogs see further than cats?
- **m** Can an elephant remember things more well than other animals?
- **n** Why have apes developed quicklier than other animals?
- **o** Can rabbits hear better than hares?

Answers

[ ] 20

GO to page 36 and check your answers.

Test it again ✓

1 Write the missing forms.

	adverb	comparative	superlative
a	slowly		
b			the most clearly
c		further	
d	badly		
e			the most politely
f	generous		
g		more	
h			the best
i		more carefully	
j	neatly		

2 Choose the best option, A or B.

a I'd like to move .... to my family.
A nearer **B** more near

b Nine o'clock? You get up .... than I do. I get up at five-thirty.
A late **B** later

c Matthew works harder .... his supervisor does.
A than **B** –

d We would all like to see you ....
A oftener **B** more often

e Can cats catch rats .... than they can catch mice?
A more easily **B** most easily

f Aim .... ! You always aim too low.
A higher **B** more high

g Joanne writes badly, but Sue writes ....
A worse **B** more badly

h Laura speaks Spanish .... than her brother does.
A more well **B** better

i Tom swims .... of all the boys in his class.
A the fastest **B** fastest

j I drive .... you do. You're a terrible driver!
A more carefully **B** more carefully than

| | 20 |

Fix it

Answers to Test it

Check your answers. Wrong answer? Read the right Fix it note to find out why.

1
- **a** the hardest → B
- **b** the most elegantly → A
- **c** worse → C
- **d** more often → A
- **e** earlier → B

2
- **a** ~~faster~~ faster than → B
- **b** correct → C
- **c** ~~more early~~ earlier → B
- **d** ~~more greedily~~ the most greedily → A
- **e** correct → B
- **f** ~~easily~~ more easily → A
- **g** ~~longer~~ longer than → D
- **h** ~~clearly~~ more clearly → A
- **i** ~~highest~~ higher → B
- **j** ~~oftener~~ more often → A
- **k** correct → A
- **l** correct → C
- **m** ~~more well~~ better → C
- **n** ~~quicklier~~ more quickly → A
- **o** ~~correct~~ → C

Now go to page 35. Test yourself again.

Answers to Test it again

1
- **a** more slowly, the most slowly
- **b** clearly, more clearly
- **c** far, the furthest
- **d** worse, the worst
- **e** politely, more politely
- **f** more generously, the most generously
- **g** much, the most
- **h** well, better
- **i** carefully, the most carefully
- **j** more neatly, the most neatly

2

a A	**b** B	**c** A	**d** B	**e** A
f A	**g** A	**h** B	**i** A	**j** B

Fix it notes

A

Make the comparative form of most adverbs by adding *more* before the adverb. Make the superlative form by adding *the most*.

B

Make the comparative form of the adverbs *early, fast, hard* and *high* by adding *er* to the adverb. Make the superlative form by adding *the* and *est*. (Change the *y* at the end of *early* to an *i* before adding *er/est*.)

C

Some adverbs, e.g. *badly, far, well,* have irregular comparative and superlative forms.

D

Use *than* after a comparative adverb.

For more information, see the Review page opposite.

Comparative and superlative adverbs

- You make the comparative form of most adverbs by adding *more* before the adverb. You make the superlative form by adding *the most.*
  quickly *more quickly* *the most quickly*

- You make the comparative form of the adverbs *early, fast, hard, high, late, low, near* and *soon* by adding *er*. You make the superlative form of these adverbs by adding *the* and *est*. You change the *y* at the end of *early* to an *i* before you add *er/est* and just add *r* and *st* to *late*.
  early *earlier* *the earliest* *fast* *faster* *the fastest*
  high *higher* *the highest* *late* *latest* *the latest*

- Some adverbs have an irregular comparative and superlative form. You need to learn these.
  far *further* *the furthest*
  well *better* *the best*
  badly *worse* *the worst*

- You use *than* after a comparative adverb.
  You finished it more quickly than I did. *She sings better than he does.*

Note: Sentences with superlative adverbs aren't as common as sentences with comparative adverbs.

Test it ✔

1 Find and correct any sentences that are wrong.

- **a** It's nearly Christmas! I'm so exciting!
- **b** The lesson was very confusing.
- **c** What an amazing party that was!
- **d** There's nothing to do here. It's a very bored town.
- **e** The film was so frightened that the kids hid behind the sofa.
- **f** Are you excited about getting married?
- **g** Bad weather can be very depressing.
- **h** I can see you're not very interesting. You're not listening to me at all.
- **i** We're all worried about Robert.
- **j** I was absolutely amazing when he gave me the flowers.

2 Choose the best option, A or B.

- **a** It's very .... when the computer doesn't work properly.
  A irritated **B** irritating
- **b** We were all .... to hear about the accident.
  A shocking **B** shocked
- **c** Are you .... that you didn't pass the exam?
  A disappointing **B** disappointed
- **d** This is a .... book about Zanzibar.
  A fascinating **B** fascinated
- **e** Stop being so ....! That's the third time I've heard that story.
  A bored **B** boring
- **f** She finds exercise extremely ....
  A tired **B** tiring
- **g** I was .... to learn about the history of the castle.
  A fascinating **B** fascinated
- **h** Why are you ....? There's a lot to do here.
  A boring **B** bored
- **i** No one seems .... in my plans.
  A interested **B** interesting
- **j** I'm sure the dog's .... He never wags his tail.
  A depressed **B** depressing

| | 20 |

GO to page 40 and check your answers.

Test it again ✔

1 Use the word at the end of each line to make a new word to fill the space.

a	I saw a dead mouse in the garden. It was ....!	DISGUST
b	What's wrong? Are you .... with me?	ANNOY
c	I'm not .... That's not very funny.	AMUSE
d	These instructions are very.. . I don't understand them.	CONFUSE
e	My parents aren't .... with my exam results.	SATISFY
f	You're .... when you're in a bad mood.	FRIGHT
g	I feel .... when I can't solve a problem.	FRUSTRATE
h	Do you find astronomy ....?	INTEREST
i	Lemon and honey is very .... when you've got a cold.	COMFORT
j	Jill was very .... about falling asleep in class.	EMBARRASS
k	That roller-coaster ride was	TERRIFY
l	I worked hard yesterday. When I got home I was	EXHAUST
m	My boss was .... when I resigned.	SURPRISE
n	Lying on the beach is very	RELAX
o	The midnight movie last night was .... It was about ghosts and vampires.	HORRIFY

2 Choose the best caption for the cartoon.

The teacher was very boring.
The teacher was very bored.

☐ 16

Fix it

Answers to Test it

Check your answers. Wrong answer? Read the right Fix it note to find out why.

1
- a ~~exciting~~ excited → A
- b correct → B
- c correct → B
- d ~~bored~~ boring → B
- e ~~frightened~~ frightening → B
- f correct → A
- g correct → B
- h ~~interesting~~ interested → A
- i correct → A
- j ~~amazing~~ amazed → A

2
- a B → B
- b B → A
- c B → A
- d A → B
- e B → B
- f B → B
- g B → A
- h B → A
- i A → A
- j A → A

Now go to page 39. Test yourself again.

Answers to Test it again

1
- a disgusting
- b annoyed
- c amused
- d confusing
- e satisfied
- f frightening
- g frustrated
- h interesting
- i comforting
- j embarrassed
- k terrifying
- l exhausted
- m surprised
- n relaxing
- o horrifying

2 The teacher was very bored.

Fix it notes

A

Use participles ending in *ed* to talk about how people feel.

B

Use participles ending in *ing* when you're describing the reason for a feeling.

For more information, see the Review page opposite.

–ing or –ed?

You can use present participles (words ending in *ing*) and past participles (words ending in *ed*) as adjectives but you need to know the difference between them. It's common for people to mix them up because they look quite similar.

Past participles used as adjectives

- You use past participles, e.g. *bored, confused, interested,* etc. as adjectives. They describe how someone feels.
  I'm bored. *You're tired.* *He's frightened.* *We're irritated.*

Present participles used as adjectives

- You use present participles, e.g. *boring, confusing, interesting,* etc. as adjectives. They describe the reason for a person's feelings.
  The film was really boring. (The film made me feel bored.)
  It was a very frightening film. (That's the reason I was frightened.)
  She finds the lessons tiring. (The lessons make her feel tired.)
  It was shocking news. (The news shocked us.)

Here's a list of common past and present participles that are used as adjectives:

amazed	amazing	frightened	frightening
amused	amusing	frustrated	frustrating
annoyed	annoying	horrified	horrifying
bored	boring	interested	interesting
comforted	comforting	irritated	irritating
confused	confusing	puzzled	puzzling
depressed	depressing	relaxed	relaxing
disappointed	disappointing	satisfied	satisfying
disgusted	disgusting	shocked	shocking
embarrassed	embarrassing	surprised	surprising
excited	exciting	terrified	terrifying
exhausted	exhausting	tired	tiring
fascinated	fascinating	worried	worrying

Countable nouns

Test it ✔

1 Find and correct ten mistakes.

a Remember to buy some potatos!

b We looked in four dictionarys but we couldn't find the word.

c There were two persons at the door.

d This film are boring – let's watch a different one.

e Look! The police is arresting the robber.

f Tom and Jill have three son – Jack, Peter and Nick.

g I'm going on a diet! My trousers doesn't fit me.

h Sam likes mouses because they're small and furry.

i Bus go up and down my street all day and they're noisy.

j In autumn the leafs fall off the trees.

2 Write the plural forms of these nouns.

a woman ....

b sheep ....

c story ....

d tooth ....

e dress ....

f tomato ....

g fox ....

h foot ....

i wolf ....

j child ....

[ ] 20

GO to page 44 and check your answers.

Test it again ✓

1 Solve the clues to complete the crossword.

Across

2 People who aren't grown up are called ....
3 Most people use these to tell the time.
6 Men have .... and women have husbands.
7 These are very young children.
9 .... cause traffic jams.
11 I'd like two .... of bread and a baguette, please.
13 These are clever animals. They steal chickens.
14 The things you bite with.

Down

1 ...., forks and spoons.
2 Almost all offices nowadays use ....
4 They're red and you eat them in salads.
5 .... are frightened of cats.
8 These vegetables grow underground.
10 There are .... in every city. They are cheaper to use than taxis.
12 People usually live in .... or apartments.

	15

Fix it

Answers to Test it

Check your answers. Wrong answer?
Read the right Fix it note to find out why.

1

a	~~potatos~~	potatoes	→ B
b	~~dictonarys~~	dictionaries	→ C
c	~~persons~~	people	→ E
d	~~are~~	is	→ F
e	~~is~~	are	→ G
f	~~son~~	sons	→ A
g	~~doesn't~~	don't	→ G
h	~~mouses~~	mice	→ E
i	~~Bus~~	Buses	→ B
j	~~leafs~~	leaves	→ D

2

a	women	→ E	**f**	tomatoes	→ B
b	sheep	→ E	**g**	foxes	→ B
c	stories	→ C	**h**	feet	→ E
d	teeth	→ E	**i**	wolves	→ D
e	dresses	→ B	**j**	children	→ E

Now go to page 43. Test yourself again.

Answers to Test it again

1

Fix it notes

A

Many English nouns are countable. Add *s* to make the plural, e.g. *boys*.

B

Add *es* to countable nouns ending in *ch, sh, s, o* and *x* to make the plural, e.g. *potatoes, dresses*.

C

To make the plural of nouns ending in consonant + *y*, change *y* to *i* and add *es*, e.g. *dictionaries*.

D

To make the plural of nouns ending in *f* or *fe*, change *f* to *v* and add *es*, e.g. *leaves, wolves*.

E

Some countable nouns are irregular. They have irregular plural forms, e.g. *people, mice, sheep, women*.

F

Use a singular verb with singular countable nouns.

G

Use a plural verb with plural nouns. Some nouns are always plural, e.g. *police, trousers*.

For more information, see the Review page opposite.

Review

Countable nouns

Spelling rules

- Many English nouns are countable. In most cases, you add *s* to the singular noun to make the plural form.
  dog/dogs *boy/boys* *shop/shops*

- If a countable noun ends in in *ch*, *sh*, *s*, *o* or *x*, you add *es* to make the plural form.
  watch/watches *brush/brushes* *bus/buses*
  potato/potatoes *fox/foxes*

- If a countable noun ends in a consonant + *y*, you change *y* to *i* and add *es*.
  dictionary/dictionaries *story/stories* *lady/ladies*

- If a countable noun ends in *f* or *fe*, you change the *f* to *v* and add *es* or *s*.
  thief/thieves *leaf/leaves* *wife/wives* *knife/knives* *life/lives*

Irregular plural forms

- Some countable nouns are irregular and therefore have irregular plural forms. You need to learn these.
  person/people *child/children* *man/men*
  woman/women *mouse/mice* *sheep/sheep*

Noun-verb agreement

- You use a singular verb with singular countable nouns.
  The child is happy. *The Oxford dictionary contains 3,500 new words.*

- You use a plural verb with plural nouns.
  The girls are swimming. *The children didn't go to school yesterday.*

- Some nouns are always plural. You use a plural verb.
  These trousers don't fit me. *Are these scissors sharp enough?*
  The police are coming. *My glasses need cleaning.*

Uncountable nouns

Test it ✔

1 Choose the best option, A or B.

- **a** Did you hear .... noise?
  A – **B** a
- **b** Rice .... good for you.
  A is **B** are
- **c** John has too much .... to do.
  A works **B** work
- **d** Can I get .... advice here?
  A an **B** –
- **e** The spaghetti you cooked .... delicious!
  A tastes **B** taste
- **f** He uses the London tube every day so he spends a lot on ....
  A travel **B** travels
- **g** We've got .... good news for you.
  A – **B** a
- **h** Money .... buy you love.
  A don't **B** doesn't
- **i** Please be quiet! You're making too much ....
  A noises **B** noise
- **j** Patrick's got .... blond hair and blue eyes.
  A a **B** –

2 Choose the correct sentence in each pair.

- **a** Three coffee, please.
- **b** Three coffees, please.

- **c** Where can I get information about the city?
- **d** Where can I get informations about the city?

- **e** This job advert says you need an experience.
- **f** This job advert says you need experience.

- **g** Oil float in water.
- **h** Oil floats in water.

- **i** Do you enjoy listening to music?
- **j** Do you enjoy listening to a music?

[ ] 15

GO to page 48 and check your answers.

Test it again ✔

1 Complete the sentences. Use a word from the list and *a* where necessary.

happiness work water coffee travel furniture luck journey tea money

a .... is expensive these days. This chair costs £150.

b Carla only drinks mineral .... She never drinks anything else.

c I wish you .... for your exams.

d .... isn't important. You can't buy happiness.

e .... grows in India and China.

f What is ....? It's difficult to describe.

g Susanna went on .... from Canada to Mexico.

h I'd like .... and a slice of cake, please.

i Nick's got .... to do so he can't come tonight.

j Christine spends £500 on .... every year.

2 Find and correct ten mistakes.

a I need money so I'm looking for a job. This advert says you must have an experience of working in an office and that you will make a progress if you are good at using a computer. I want an information about the salary but it doesn't say anything about pay.

b We'd like an orange juice and two coffee, please.

Certainly, would you like a milk and sugar?

c SHOPPING
an orange juice
teas
milks
butter
bread
fruits
water
a coffee

☐ 20

Fix it

Answers to Test it

Check your answers. Wrong answer? Read the right Fix it note to find out why.

1
- a B → D
- b A → B
- c B → A
- d B → C
- e A → B
- f A → A
- g A → C
- h B → B
- i B → D
- j B → C

2 The correct sentences are:
- b → D
- c → A
- f → C
- h → B
- i → C.

Now go to page 47. Test yourself again.

Answers to Test it again

1
- a Furniture
- b water
- c luck
- d Money
- e Tea
- f happiness
- g a journey
- h a coffee
- i work
- j travel

2
- a ~~an experience~~ experience
  ~~a progress~~ progress
  ~~an information~~ information
- b ~~coffee~~ coffees
  ~~a sugar~~ sugar
- c ~~an orange juice~~ orange juice
  ~~teas~~ tea
  ~~milks~~ milk
  ~~fruits~~ fruit
  ~~a coffee~~ coffee

Fix it notes

A

Uncountable nouns are normally singular. Don't add *s*.

B

Use a singular verb with uncountable nouns.

C

Don't use *a* or *an* with uncountable nouns.

D

Some nouns, e.g. *coffee*, *noise*, can be countable or uncountable with different meanings.

For more information, see the Review page opposite.

Review

Uncountable nouns

Many nouns that are uncountable in English are countable in some other languages. You need to learn whether a noun is countable or uncountable when you see it for the first time. For information about using quantifiers with uncountable nouns, see page 53.

- Uncountable nouns, e.g. *advice, information, milk, petrol, sugar,* etc. are normally singular. They don't have a plural form so you can't add *s* to the noun.
  advice NOT ~~*advices*~~ *information* NOT ~~*informations*~~
  milk NOT ~~*milks*~~ *petrol* NOT ~~*petrols*~~

- You use a singular verb with an uncountable noun.
  Milk tastes nice. *Apple juice is sweet.* *The water feels cold.*

- You don't use the articles *a* or *an* with uncountable nouns.
  This is hard work. NOT ~~*a hard work*~~
  I need information. NOT ~~*an information*~~
  Do you want advice? NOT ~~*an advice*~~

- Some nouns can be countable or uncountable but be careful! The meaning changes.
  Did you hear a noise? (a particular noise)
  There's too much noise. I can't work. (noise in general)

  I'd like a coffee, please. (a cup of coffee)
  We need coffee and sugar. (coffee and sugar in general)

  There's a hair on your jacket. (just one hair)
  He's got blond hair. (the hair on his head)

- Here's a list of common uncountable nouns:

accommodation
advice
baggage
bread
butter
cheese
coffee
electricity
experience
fruit
furniture
gas
hair
happiness
information
juice
knowledge
love
luck
luggage
milk
money
noise
music
news
oil
petrol
pollution
progress
rice
spaghetti
sugar
tea
traffic
travel
water
weather
work

Quantifiers: *some, any, much* and *many*

Test it ✔

1 Choose the correct sentence in each pair.

a Jim's got any photos to show me.
b Jim's got some photos to show me.

c I don't think there's any coffee.
d I don't think there's some coffee.

e Can I have some more cheese, please?
f Can I have any more cheese, please?

g Jo doesn't have many trouble making friends.
h Jo doesn't have much trouble making friends.

i I don't know much French.
j I don't know many French.

k We don't eat much sweet things.
l We don't eat many sweet things.

m Have we got any milk left?
n Have we got some milk left?

o Look! Here's any information about the city.
p Look! Here's some information about the city.

q How much time have you got?
r How many time have you got?

s There aren't some apples.
t There aren't any apples.

2 Choose the best option.

a We haven't got much/many time.
b Would you like some/any bread?
c How much/many times have you been to Egypt?
d George doesn't like many vegetable/vegetables.
e Pete's bought some/any CDs.

☐ 15

GO to page 52 and check your answers.

Test it again ✔

1 Choose the correct option, A or B.

a Can I have .... apple juice?
A any **B** some

b Do you play .... sports?
A any **B** much

c Sam doesn't want .... milk. He wants water.
A any **B** some

d How .... legs has a millipede got?
A much **B** many

e I didn't get .... answers right. All the questions were too hard.
A any **B** some

f There .... much butter left.
A is **B** isn't

g We didn't see .... pollution in Kathmandu.
A much **B** many

h Clara has got .... interesting books.
A much **B** some

i Have you got any ....?
A stamp **B** stamps

j There .... any wolves in England.
A are **B** aren't

2 Complete the sentences. Use *much, many, some* or *any*. Sometimes more than one answer may be correct.

a Bill needs .... advice. Can you help him?

b Have you got .... friends?

c Is there .... bread? I'm hungry.

d How .... petrol is there in the car?

e Pat bought .... books and a DVD.

f I need .... more time.

g There isn't .... time, so hurry up!

h How .... cents are there in €7?

i You didn't buy .... clothes today, did you?

j We took .... photos when we were in Venice.

	20

Fix it

Answers to Test it

Check your answers. Wrong answer? Read the right Fix it note to find out why.

1 The correct sentences are:

b → A		l → E	
c → C		m → C	
e → B		p → A	
h → D		q → D	
i → D		t → C	

2
- **a** much → D
- **b** some → B
- **c** many → E
- **d** vegetables → E
- **e** some → A

Now go to page 51. Test yourself again.

Answers to Test it again

1
a B **b** A **c** A **d** B **e** A
f B **g** A **h** B **i** B **j** B

2
- **a** some
- **b** any/many
- **c** any
- **d** much
- **e** some
- **f** some
- **g** any/much
- **h** many
- **i** any/many
- **j** some

Fix it notes

A
Use *some* in positive sentences with uncountable nouns and plural nouns when you're talking about a small amount or number.

B
Use *some* in questions when you expect the answer to be 'yes'.

C
Use *any* in negative sentences and in most questions with uncountable nouns and plural nouns when you're talking about a small amount or number.

D
Use *much* and *how much* with uncountable nouns.

E
Use *many* and *how many* with plural nouns.

For more information, see the Review page opposite.

Review

Quantifiers: *some, any, much* and *many*

Some

- You use *some* with uncountable nouns and plural nouns when you're talking about a small amount or number and you don't know or it isn't important to know the exact amount.
  We need some information. *He's got some new books.*

- You use *some* in positive sentences, not in negative sentences.
  There are some letters on the table. NOT ~~*There aren't some letters on the table.*~~

- You use *some* in questions when you expect the answer to be 'yes'.
  Can I have some cheese? *Do you want some help?*

Any

- You use *any* with uncountable nouns and plural nouns when you're talking about a small amount or number.
  There isn't any milk. *Are there any rooms for tonight?*

- You use *any* in negative sentences and in most questions. You don't use *any* in positive sentences.
  He doesn't like any of the colours. NOT ~~*He does like any of the colours.*~~
  Do you like any of these paintings?

Much

- You use *much* with uncountable nouns in negative sentences, not in positive sentences.
  There isn't much butter left. NOT ~~*There is much butter left.*~~

- You use *much* (or *how much*) with uncountable nouns in questions.
  Is there much coffee left?
  How much time is there before the film starts?

Many

- You use *many* with plural nouns in negative sentences, not in positive sentences.
  Sheila hasn't got many DVDs. NOT ~~*Sheila's got many DVDs.*~~

- You use *many* (or *how many*) with plural nouns in questions.
  Are there many mountains in Scotland?
  How many times have you been to Italy?

Something, anybody, nowhere, everything, etc.

Test it ✔

1 Choose the correct option.

a I don't know nobody/anybody.
b Everything are/is perfect.
c Are you sure you've looked somewhere/everywhere?
d Nobody/Anybody wants to help me.
e There isn't something/anything wrong.
f She doesn't like anybody/somebody who laughs at her.
g Did you say anything/nothing to Jenny?
h We didn't go anywhere/somewhere last weekend.
i Everybody look/looks very cheerful today.
j Peter can see anybody/somebody through the window.

2 Complete the sentences. Use one word in each space.

a I looked .... for my wallet but I couldn't find it.
b There's .... at the door. Could you see who it is?
c Has .... heard of the poet Polly Clark?
d .... ever listens to me.
e .... told me. I can't remember who.
f 'Where are you going?' '.. . I'm staying here.'
g Bill needs .... to stay for the night.
h We've got .... to eat. Let's order a pizza.
i Well done! .... passed the exam.
j Is there .... to drink? I'm thirsty.

[ ] 20

GO to page 56 and check your answers.

Test it again ✔

1 Choose the best option, A or B.

a Is .... at home?
A somebody **B** anybody

b .... is more beautiful than this lovely beach.
A Everywhere **B** Nowhere

c I feel sorry for John. He's not very good at ....
A anything **B** something

d Come here. I want to tell you ....
A anything **B** something

e Is .... ready?
A everything **B** nothing

f He's very lucky. There's .... he needs.
A anything **B** nothing

g You must have left your umbrella ....
A somewhere **B** everywhere

h .... is allowed to speak during the lecture.
A anybody **B** nobody

i Don't worry. Everything .... going to be OK.
A are **B** is

j .... Sue goes, David follows.
A Nowhere **B** Everywhere

k Do we need to bring ....?
A anything **B** something

2 Choose the best caption for the cartoon.

I just don't understand why everybody likes me.
I just don't understand why nobody likes me.
I just don't understand why anybody likes me.

[ ] 12

Fix it

Answers to Test it

Check your answers. Wrong answer? Read the right Fix it note to find out why.

1 a anybody → B
b is → E
c everywhere → D
d Nobody → C
e anything → B
f anybody → B
g anything → B
h anywhere → B
i looks → E
j somebody → A

2 a everywhere → D
b somebody → A
c anybody → B
d Nobody → C
e Somebody → A
f Nowhere → C
g somewhere → A
h nothing → C
i Everybody → D
j anything → B

Now go to page 55. Test yourself again.

Answers to Test it again

1 a B b B c A d B e A
f B g A h B i B j B
k A

2 I just don't understand why nobody likes me.

Fix it notes

A

Use *something*, *somewhere* and *somebody* in positive sentences.

B

Use *anything*, *anywhere* and *anybody* in questions and negative sentences.

C

Use *nothing*, *nowhere* and *nobody* in positive sentences.

D

Use *everything*, *everywhere* and *everybody* in positive sentences, negative sentences and in questions.

E

Use a singular verb with *everything*, *everywhere* and *everybody*.

For more information, see the Review page opposite.

Review

Something, anybody, nowhere, everything, etc.

You can make compound words using *some, any, no* and *every* with *thing, body* and *where.* Although *body* is used in this unit (*somebody, anybody, nobody, everybody*), you can also use *one* (*someone, anyone, no one, everyone*). The meaning is the same.

- You use *something, somewhere*, and *somebody* in positive sentences.
  There's something wrong. *Let's go out somewhere.*
  Somebody has borrowed my dictionary.

  Note: You can use *something, somewhere* and *somebody* in questions when you expect the answer to be 'yes'.
  Did you say something? *Did you find somewhere to stay last night?*
  Is there somebody you can talk to?

- You use *anything, anywhere* and *anybody* in negative sentences and in questions.
  There isn't anything to do in this town. *I don't want to go anywhere today.*
  Is anybody listening to me?

- You use *nothing, nowhere* and *nobody* in positive sentences.
  We have nothing to declare. *'Where have you been?' 'Nowhere.'*
  There's nobody at home.

- You use *everything, everywhere* and *everybody* in positive and negative sentences, and also in questions.
  Everything is fine. *No, I haven't looked everywhere yet.*
  Is everybody happy?

- Be careful! You use a singular verb (not a plural verb) with *everything, everywhere* and *everybody.*
  Everything tastes delicious. *Almost everywhere in Egypt is interesting.*
  Everybody is delighted with the plans.

Both, all; each, every; either, neither

Test it

1 Choose the best option.

- **a** I've met Steve twice. Every/Each time he's been quite rude to me.
- **b** Each student/students bought a dictionary and a grammar book.
- **c** All/Both Jupiter and Mars are planets.
- **d** Kate doesn't like either/neither of the books we gave her.
- **e** Dogs, cats, rabbits – Jimmy loves both/all of them.
- **f** Some people can't eat nuts and some can't eat wheat either/neither.
- **g** I've seen this film at least ten times. I like it more every times/time.
- **h** Every/Each parking space in the town was full so we went home.
- **i** Both of the child/children got ten out of ten in their tests.
- **j** There were about fifty people at the party and they were both/all dancing.

2 Complete the sentences. Use *both, all, each, every, either* or *neither*.

- **a** .... of my kids go to the same school. Theo is in Class 3 and Rosie is in Class 1.
- **b** My husband likes peaches and I like apricots, but .... of us likes plums.
- **c** .... boy in the class passed the exam.
- **d** Sheila read two books by Martin Amis but she didn't enjoy .... of them.
- **e** .... animals need water in order to live.
- **f** Mary had two bridesmaids at her wedding. .... girl carried a bouquet of roses.
- **g** .... person in the audience stood up and clapped when the play ended.
- **h** .... of Sam's two children likes eggs.
- **i** Shall I buy the red one or the blue one? I really like them ....
- **j** .... members of the leisure club must carry their membership cards.

[ ] 20

GO to page 60 and check your answers.

Test it again

1 Choose the best option, A or B.

a Lobsters, crabs, oysters, mussels – they're .... delicious!
A all **B** both

b .... man admitted burgling the flat.
A Both **B** Neither

c .... suspects denied being in the area.
A Neither **B** Both

d Charlie looks happier and happier every ....
A day **B** days

e I've enjoyed .... holiday I've ever been on.
A each **B** every

f Daniel could live in Paris or London but he doesn't like .... of them.
A neither **B** either

g Each of the .... we stayed in had a swimming pool.
A hotels **B** hotel

h 'Coffee or tea?' 'I don't mind – I'll have ....'
A neither **B** either

i .... of you like pasta, don't you?
A Every **B** All

j .... of us go to the gym three times a week.
A Every of us **B** Both of us

2 Write new sentences with similar meanings. Use *both, all, every, either* or *neither*.

a He likes the Porsche and the Ferrari.
He likes .... cars.

b Tom doesn't read *The Times* or *The Sun*.
Tom doesn't read .... of those newspapers.

c Lucy forgot her English book, her Maths book and her History book.
Lucy forgot .... her books.

d We invited Beth and Judy to dinner but they didn't come.
We invited Beth and Judy but .... of them came.

e He wears a different tie on Monday, Tuesday, Wednesday, Thursday and Friday.
He wears a different tie .... day of the week.

| | 15 |

Fix it

Answers to Test it

Check your answers. Wrong answer? Read the right Fix it note to find out why.

1 **a** Each → C, D
b student → C
c Both → A
d either → E
e all → B
f either → E
g time → D
h Every → D
i children → F
j all → B

2 **a** Both → F
b neither → F
c Every → D
d either → F, E
e All → B
f Each → C
g Every → D
h Neither → F, E
i both → A
j All → B

Now go to page 59. Test yourself again.

Answers to Test it again

1 **a** A **b** B **c** B **d** A **e** B
f B **g** A **h** B **i** B **j** B

2 **a** both
b either
c all
d neither
e every

Fix it notes

A
Use *both* to talk about two things when you mean one thing *and* the other thing.

B
Use *all* to talk about three or more things. Use *all* with a plural noun or pronoun.

C
Use *each* when you're talking about two or more things. Put it before a singular noun.

D
Use *every* when you're talking about three or more things. Put it before a singular noun.

E
Use *either* in negative sentences.
Use *neither* in positive sentences.

F
Use *both of, each of, either of,* and *neither of* before a plural noun or pronoun.

For more information, see the Review page opposite.

Review

Both, all; each, every; either, neither

- Use *both* to talk about two things when you mean one thing **and** the other thing.
  Both Algeria and Morocco are in North Africa. *Both my children like fish.*

- You use *all* with a plural noun or pronoun to talk about three or more things.
  All living things need oxygen. *All my friends are wonderful.*
  You're all crazy!

- You use *each* when you're talking about two or more things. It goes before a singular noun.
  Each time I've seen him, he's been very kind to me. (I've seen him at least twice.)
  Pete's decided to go running each day for a week.

- You use *every* to talk about three or more things. It goes before a singular noun.
  Every letter you write is beautiful!
  Paula wins the competition every year.

  Note: Often you can use *each* or *every* without changing the meaning of the sentence.
  I love you more each/every day.
  As a general rule to help you decide which to use, you usually use *each* when you're thinking of things separately. You use *every* when you're thinking of things as a group.

- You use *either* in negative sentences (not in positive sentences). *Either* means one thing or the other thing.
  Gemma didn't like either of the dresses I bought.
  (She didn't like the black dress. She didn't like the white dress.)
  NOT ~~*Gemma liked either of the dresses I bought.*~~

- You use *neither* in positive sentences (not in negative sentences).
  Neither means not one thing or the other thing.
  Neither of my brothers remembered my birthday.
  (My brother John didn't remember. My brother James didn't remember.)
  NOT ~~*Neither of my brothers didn't remember my birthday.*~~

- You use *both of, each of, either of,* and *neither of* before a plural noun or before a pronoun.
  'Which do you prefer?' 'I like both of them.'
  There were two small dogs. Each of the dogs was wearing a red collar.
  Steve met Vic and David but he didn't like either of them.
  Neither of my two best friends likes going to the cinema.

Possessives

Test it ✔

1 Choose the best sentence in each pair.

a This is my brother's wife.
b This is the wife of my brother.

c The government should listen to the peoples' problems.
d The government should listen to the people's problems.

e What's the babies' name?
f What's the baby's name?

g The roof of the house needs to be mended.
h The house's roof needs to be mended.

i Isn't that the mother of Sylvia?
j Isn't that Sylvia's mother?

k Johns' leg is broken.
l John's leg is broken.

m Buster is Steve's and Liz's dog.
n Buster is Steve and Liz's dog.

o Frances writes children's books.
p Frances writes childrens' books.

q I love the Italian's passion for good food.
r I love the Italians' passion for good food.

s Lady's clothes are on the second floor.
t Ladies' clothes are on the second floor.

2 Choose the best option, A or B.

a There is something wrong with ....
A the ear of the rabbit **B** the rabbit's ear
b I can't wear that! It's a .... jacket!
A girls' **B** girl's
c .... and Janet's son is working in Canada for a year.
A Charles **B** Charles's
d Don't put your fingers in the .... cage! They'll bite you.
A monkeys' **B** monkey's
e What was .... we watched last night?
A the name of the film **B** the film's name

☐ 15

GO to page 64 and check your answers.

Test it again

1 Write possessive forms.

a Jim and Jane/dog ....
b the boys/books ....
c the people/choice ....
d Helen/house ....
e the cupboard/door ....
f my friends/problems ....
g her parents/car ....
h the men/department ....
i the puppies/basket ....
j bookcase/shelf ....

2 Find and correct the mistakes in the story.

The thieves broke into number 42 Acacia Avenue at the day's end. The house's alarm system wasn't working, unfortunately, so they managed to spend a long time inside. They stole Julie's grandfathers' gold watch and her parent's collection of valuable paintings. They smashed a window at the house's front to get into the building and escaped by breaking down the back door. Julies' children were very upset and frightened when they returned home from school.

| | 15 |

Fix it

Answers to Test it

Check your answers. Wrong answer? Read the right Fix it note to find out why.

1 The best sentences are:

a	→ D	l	→ A
d	→ C	n	→ F
f	→ A	o	→ C
g	→ E	r	→ B
j	→ D	t	→ B

2 a B → D
b B → A
c A → F
d A → B
e A → E

Now go to page 63. Test yourself again.

Answers to Test it again

1 **a** Jim and Jane's dog
b the boys' books
c the people's choice
d Helen's house
e the door of the cupboard
f my friends' problems
g her parent's car
h the men's department
i the puppies' basket
j the shelf of the bookcase

2

~~the day's end~~	the end of the day
~~grandfathers'~~	grandfather's
~~parent's~~	parents'
~~the house's front~~	the front of the house
~~Julies'~~	Julie's

Fix it notes

A
Add *'s* (apostrophe + *s*) to singular nouns to make the possessive form.

B
Add *'* (apostrophe) to plural nouns to make the possessive form.

C
Add *'s* (apostrophe + *s*) to irregular plurals to make the possessive form.

D
Use *'s* (apostrophe + *s*) to make the possessive form with a person or an animal.

E
Use *of* + *the* to make the possessive form with something that isn't a person or an animal, e.g. *the roof of the house*.

F
Only put *'s* (apostrophe + *s*) after the second noun in a pair of nouns, e.g. *Steve and Liz's dog*.

For more information, see the Review page opposite.

Possessives

- You add *'s* (apostrophe + *s*) to singular nouns to make the possessive form.
  John's friends (the friends John's got)
  the dog's bone (the bone the dog's got)

- You add *'* (apostrophe) to plural nouns to make the possessive form.
  the boys' bikes   *the girls' school*   *the kids' uniforms*
  my friends' problems   *my parents' house*

- You add *'s* (apostrophe + *s*) to irregular plurals to make the possessive form.
  children's stories   *men's hobbies*
  women's interest   *people's fears*

- You use *'s* (apostrophe + *s*) to make the possessive form when you're talking about something that belongs to a person or an animal.
  the rabbit's ear NOT ~~*the ear of the rabbit*~~
  the child's toy   *my brother's son*

- You use *of* + *the* to make the possessive form with other nouns.
  the end of the day NOT ~~*the day's end*~~   *the leg of the chair*

- You only use *'s* once, even if there is more than one noun. You don't put *'s* after both nouns.
  John and Barbara's car NOT ~~*John's and Barbara's*~~
  Harry and Sally's friends

Prepositions of time: *at, on, in*

Test it ✔

1 Complete the sentences. Use *in, on* or *at*.

- **a** I'm seeing the doctor .... Friday morning.
- **b** Jack woke up .... the night. He had a bad dream.
- **c** Fenelon Castle was built .... the fourteenth century.
- **d** What are you doing .... lunchtime?
- **e** It's very nice here .... the autumn.
- **f** Come and see me .... half-past two.
- **g** Let's meet up .... Easter.
- **h** Nick often works .... night.
- **i** Where will you be .... New Year's Eve?
- **j** I'm going on holiday .... the first week of July.

2 Correct the mistakes in the instant message conversation.

- **a** Cookie says: What are you doing on tomorrow?
- **b** Cricket says: I'm busy. I've got a meeting on 11.30.
- **c** Cookie says: Do you fancy going out at Friday?
- **d** Cricket says: No, I can't. I'm working on the evening that day.
- **e** Cookie says: Oh, OK. What are you doing on the weekend then?
- **f** Cricket says: Well, there's a football match in Saturday afternoon.
- **g** Cookie says: How about meeting on the morning?
- **h** Cricket says: No, sorry. It's the 15th. I have a meeting at the 15th of every month.
- **i** Cookie says: Are you free at all at December?
- **j** Cricket says: Not really. I don't go out much on the winter.
- **k** Cookie says: Where will you be in Christmas?
- **l** Cricket says: At Christmas Day, we're going to my parents. We go every year.
- **m** Cookie says: So you're not free on next week?
- **n** Cricket says: No. I'm afraid not. And actually in next year I'm pretty busy too.
- **o** Cookie says: You said the same thing on last year!

A

Send

☐ 25

GO to page 68 and check your answers.

Test it again

1 Choose the best option, A or B.

a My appointment is .... 10.20 tomorrow.
A at **B** on

b Do you go to church .... Easter?
A at **B** in

c We're having a party .... New Year's Eve.
A at **B** on

d Are you free .... 11 June?
A – **B** on

e Paddy was born .... 1970.
A on **B** in

f I woke up three times .... the night.
A in **B** at

g Let's go shopping .... the morning.
A on **B** in

h She has her hair cut .... every month.
A – **B** in

i Montaigne lived .... the sixteenth century.
A – **B** in

j I often have good ideas .... night.
A in **B** at

2 Put in a preposition where necessary.

a Quite a lot of people get depressed .... the winter.

b Jo's seeing his boss .... this afternoon.

c We're going to a nightclub .... Saturday evening.

d Will you come for lunch .... Christmas Eve?

e I always get up .... 5.30 a.m.

f It's very quiet here .... night.

g Let's meet up .... the second week of September.

h No one saw Mike .... last week.

i They test the fire alarm .... Monday mornings.

j I met a very nice man .... the weekend.

	20

Fix it

Answers to Test it

Check your answers. Wrong answer? Read the right Fix it note to find out why.

1
- **a** on → D
- **b** in → F
- **c** in → E
- **d** at → A
- **e** in → E
- **f** at → A
- **g** at → B
- **h** at → A
- **i** on → C
- **j** in → E

2
- **a** ~~on~~ – → G
- **b** ~~on~~ at → A
- **c** ~~at~~ on → D
- **d** ~~on~~ in → F
- **e** ~~on~~ at → B
- **f** ~~in~~ on → D
- **g** ~~on~~ in → F
- **h** ~~at~~ on → D
- **i** ~~at~~ in → E
- **j** ~~on~~ in → E
- **k** ~~in~~ at → B
- **l** ~~At~~ On → C
- **m** ~~on~~ – → G
- **n** ~~in~~ – → G
- **o** ~~on~~ – → G

Now go to page 67. Test yourself again.

Answers to Test it again

1
- **a** A **b** A **c** B **d** B **e** B
- **f** A **g** B **h** A **i** B **j** B

2
- **a** in
- **b** –
- **c** on
- **d** on
- **e** at
- **f** at
- **g** in
- **h** –
- **i** on
- **j** at

Fix it notes

A
Use *at* with clock times, times of the day and with the expression *at night*.

B
Use *at* with *the weekend* and festivals when you're talking about the whole period of time.

C
Use *on* when you're talking about one particular day in a festival, e.g. *on New Year's Eve, on Easter Sunday*.

D
Use *on* with days of the week, dates and expressions like *Friday morning, Saturday afternoon*.

E
Use *in* with months, years, centuries, seasons and with the expression *the first/second/third/last week*.

F
Use *in* with expressions like *in the morning/afternoon/evening*. Also use *in* with the expression *in the night* when you're talking about a particular night, usually the night before.

G
Don't use a preposition before expressions like *last year, next year, next week, tomorrow*.

For more information, see the Review page opposite.

Review

Prepositions of time: *at, on, in*

At

- You use *at* with all clock times, times of the day and with the expression *at night.*
  The appointment is at 10.20. *I'll see you at lunchtime.*
  Tony works best at night.

- You use *at* with weekends and festivals when you're talking about the holiday as a whole period of time.
  Did you have fun at the weekend? (All weekend.)
  What are you doing at Christmas? (The whole of the Christmas period.)

On

- You use *on* when you're talking about one particular day during a festival.
  There's a great film on TV on Christmas Day.
  Do you eat chocolate eggs on Easter Sunday?

- You use *on* with days of the week, dates, and with expressions like *on Monday morning, on Sunday evening,* etc.
  Kate's baby was born on Friday. *His birthday is on 4 October.*
  Are you doing anything on Tuesday evening?

In

- You use *in* with months, years, centuries, seasons and with the expression *the first/second/third/last week.*
  The weather's great in August. *I bought the house in 2002.*
  Columbus went to America in the fifteenth century.
  We have our main holiday in the summer.
  The meeting's in the third week of April.

- You use *in* with expressions like *in the morning/afternoon/evening,* and with the expression *in the night* when you're talking about a particular night (usually the night before).
  See you in the morning! *I had a horrible dream in the night.*

No preposition

- You don't use a preposition with expressions of time like *every year, last night, next month, this week, today, tomorrow, yesterday,* etc.
  We see each other every week. *Where did you go last night?*
  Next month I'm going to Nepal. *Let's meet tomorrow.*

Prepositions of place: *in, on, at*

Test it ✔

1 Choose the best option.

a Catherine's in/at the United States at the moment.
b What's that black thing in/on the ceiling?
c 'I can see Tom in the garden but where's George?' 'He's at/in the cinema.'
d Have you read the article in/on page 16?
e Get the 9.15 train from Paddington and change at/in Oxford.
f Can you call back later? Myles isn't on/at his desk right now.
g Cool! I've just found €20 in/at the pocket of my jeans.
h The ancient town of Luxor is in/on the Nile.
i He left all his shopping on/in the bus.
j Your homework's still on/in the car.

2 Complete the sentences. Use *in, on* or *at*.

a Guess who I met .... the train?
b Please put the books back .... the shelf.
c Turn left .... the traffic lights.
d She's lived .... this village for about ten years.
e Who's that .... the door?
f Help! There's a spider .... the wall!
g Kenya is .... the equator, isn't it?
h There's a funny mark .... the carpet.
i Mum's .... the supermarket. She'll be back by four.
j Luckily no one was .... the ship when it sank.

[ ] 20

GO to page 72 and check your answers.

Test it again

1 Match the two halves of each sentence. Add *in*, *on* or *at*.

a	There's some milk	1	.... the waiting room.
b	Please buy some aspirin	2	.... Singapore?
c	Turn right	3	.... the river Ganges.
d	I left the dogs	4	.... the chemist's.
e	Billy's	5	.... a busy road so it's quite noisy.
f	My house is	6	.... school. He'll be home at four.
g	There are three patients	7	.... the car.
h	He spends a lot of time	8	.... the crossroads and go straight on.
i	The city of Varanasi is	9	.... the fridge.
j	How long have you lived	10	.... planes and trains.

2 Find the incorrect sentences.

a The documents are in the drawer.

b I read the newspaper in the bus.

c You'll find the author's name in the cover.

d Look! There's a cat on the roof.

e Katie was lying on the grass staring at the sky.

f I'm in the garden.

g What's that in your computer screen?

h Why isn't the dog on his basket?

i He felt OK once he was on the plane.

j Of course Rome is in the river Tiber!

/20

Fix it

Answers to Test it

Check your answers. Wrong answer?
Read the right Fix it note to find out why.

1

a in → A	**f** at → E
b on → B	**g** in → A
c at → F	**h** on → C
d on → B	**i** on → D
e at → E	**j** in → A

2

a on → D	**f** on → B
b on → B	**g** on → C
c at → E	**h** on → B
d in → A	**i** at → F
e at → E	**j** on → D

Now go to page 71. Test yourself again.

Answers to Test it again

1

a 9 in	**f** 5 on
b 4 at	**g** 1 in
c 8 at	**h** 10 on
d 7 in	**i** 3 on
e 6 at	**j** 2 in

2

a correct
b ~~in~~ on
c ~~in~~ on
d correct
e correct
f correct
g ~~in~~ on
h ~~on~~ in
i correct
j ~~in~~ on

Fix it notes

A
Use *in* for three-dimensional spaces, e.g. pockets, rooms, buildings, villages, countries, cars.

B
Use *on* for two-dimensional surfaces, e.g. pages of a book, walls, ceilings, carpets, tables, shelves.

C
Use *on* to talk about places on a line, e.g. *on the Nile, on the equator*.

D
Use *on* to talk about buses, trains, planes and ships (but not cars).

E
Use *at* for one-dimensional points or positions, e.g. *at a desk, at the door, at the traffic lights*. Also use *at* when you're talking about points on a journey, e.g. *at Oxford*.

F
Use *at* for buildings when you're thinking about what people do inside them, e.g. *at the cinema* (watching a film), *at the supermarket* (doing the shopping), *at Mary's house* (for a party).

For more information, see the Review page opposite.

Review

Prepositions of place: *in, on, at*

In

- You use *in* to talk about spaces that are three-dimensional, like boxes, drawers, cupboards, rooms, houses, cities, countries, etc.
  What's in the box? *The letters are in the top drawer.*
  Put the salt back in the cupboard, please. *I'm in the kitchen.*
  He lives in Oxford. *How long have they been in France?*
  Your glasses are in the car.

On

- You use *on* to talk about two-dimensional surfaces, like the pages of a book, TV or computer screens, walls, ceilings, shelves, tables, beaches, grass, etc.
  It's on page 237. *Hang the picture on the wall.*
  What's that mark on the ceiling? *I love lying on the beach.*
  The rabbit's sitting on the grass.

- You use *on* to talk about the position of something on a line, e.g. a road or a river.
  My house is on a busy street. *London is on the river Thames.*
  Ecuador is on the equator.

- You also use *on* to talk about many methods of transport including buses, trains, planes, ships, bicycles, horses, etc. Note, however, that you don't use *on* for cars, you use *in*.
  I left my homework on the bus. *We'll get a coffee on the train.*
  Malcolm cycled from Leeds to London on his bike.

At

- You use *at* to talk about one-dimensional points or positions in space. Often these are points on a journey or places to meet.
  The coach stops at Edinburgh and Glasgow. *Turn right at the traffic lights.*
  See you at the bus stop.

- You use *at* to talk about buildings or places when you're thinking about what people do inside them.
  Mum's at the supermarket. *We met at Nick's house.*
  Let's meet at the restaurant. *I'll drop you at the station.*

Note: There's a change in meaning when you use *in* or *at*.
'Where were you?' 'I was at the theatre.' (watching a play)
It was very cold in the theatre last night. (inside the theatre)

Questions

Test it ✓

1 Find one correct question. Correct the other nine.

a Like you red wine?

b Tom's hurt himself.
What did happen?

c When you will be back?
About five o'clock.

d Is watching John TV?

e Who you saw?

f Who saw you?
Nobody.

g Do you can tell me the time?

h Did she to go to Mexico?
Yes, I think so.

i How much this costs?

j Why Dan isn't here?
I don't know.

2 Write questions. Use the words given and one other word in the right order.

	Questions	Answers
a	'where you going?'	'To the bank.'
b	'broke the window?'	'Freddy.'
c	'you meet who?'	'Tony and Richard.'
d	'you speak Greek?'	'Yes, a little.'
e	'where did you?'	'I went to Rome.'
f	'are coming?'	'Yes, I am.'
g	'does he want to see?'	'He wants to see Jo.'
h	'we be late?'	'No, we won't.'
i	'who did you.'	'I told Nick and Sam.'
j	'Jo play tennis?'	'Yes, I think so.'

[ ] 20

GO to page 76 and check your answers.

Test it again ✔

1 Put the letters of the words in the right order. Use the words to complete the questions.

SHA ☐☐☐ TAWH ☐☐☐☐ IDD ☐☐☐ OWH ☐☐☐ SI ☐☐
KELI ☐☐☐☐ WOH ☐☐☐ DESO ☐☐☐☐ NAC ☐☐☐
WYH ☐☐☐ LILW ☐☐☐☐

a .... is Keith doing?
b Who .... you meet at the party yesterday?
c .... Jenny ready?
d Do you .... coffee or do you prefer tea?
e .... said that?
f .... do you pronounce this word?
g .... this shirt look good on me?
h When .... you go to Chamonix – next month or in June?
i How many languages .... you speak?
j .... did you do that? You must be crazy.
k .... Dad found his keys yet?

2 Choose the best caption for the cartoon.

Supper is ready, darling?
Is supper ready, darling?
Is ready supper, darling?

☐ 12

Fix it

Answers to Test it

Check your answers. Wrong answer? Read the right Fix it note to find out why.

1 The correct sentence is f.

- **a** Do you like red wine? → C
- **b** What happened? → F
- **c** When will you be back? → A
- **d** Is John watching TV? → B
- **e** Who did you see? → C
- **f** correct → F
- **g** Can you tell me the time? → D
- **h** Did she go to Mexico? → E
- **i** How much does this cost? → C
- **j** Why isn't Dan here? → A

2
- **a** Where are you going? → A
- **b** Who broke the window? → F
- **c** Who did you meet? → C
- **d** Do you speak Greek? → A
- **e** Where did you go? → E
- **f** Are you coming? → B
- **g** Who does he want to see? → G
- **h** Will we be late? → A
- **i** Who did you tell? → E
- **j** Does Jo play tennis? → C

Now go to page 75. Test yourself again.

Answers to Test it again

1
- **a** What
- **b** did
- **c** Is
- **d** like
- **e** Who
- **f** How
- **g** Does
- **h** will
- **i** can
- **j** Why
- **k** Has

2 Is supper ready, darling?

Fix it notes

A

Put auxiliary verbs, e.g. *be, do, have*, and modal verbs, e.g. *can, must, will*, before (not after) the subject in a question.

B

Only put the auxiliary verb, e.g. *be, do, have*, before the subject in a question. Don't put the whole verb before the subject.

C

If there isn't an auxiliary verb in the question, use *do, does* or *did.*

D

You don't need *do, does* or *did* if there's already an auxiliary or modal verb in the question.

E

Use the base form of the verb (not the infinitive) after *do, does,* or *did* in a question.

F

When a question word, e.g. *who, what, where*, is the subject of a question, put it before the verb. Don't use *do*.

G

When a question word, e.g. *who, what, where*, is the object of a question, use normal question word order with *do, does* or *did.*

For more information, see the Review page opposite.

Review

Questions

- You put auxiliary verbs e.g. *be, do, have* and modal verbs, e.g. *can, will, should* before (not after) the subject in a question.
  Do you want some help? NOT ~~*You do want some help?*~~
  When will you be back? NOT ~~*When you will be back?*~~

- You only put the auxiliary verb e.g. *be, do, have* before the subject. You don't put the whole verb before the subject.
  When are Patrick and Isabelle coming? NOT ~~*When are coming ...*~~
  Where have you been? NOT ~~*Where have been you?*~~

- If the question hasn't got an auxiliary verb, you use *do, does* or *did.*
  Do you like travelling? NOT ~~*Like you travelling?*~~
  Does Martin enjoy his work? NOT ~~*Enjoys Martin his work?*~~
  Did they ring you last night? NOT ~~*Rang you they last night?*~~

- You don't need to use *do, does* or *did* if there's already an auxiliary or modal verb in the question.
  Have you been to Singapore? NOT ~~*Do you have been ...*~~
  Can you see Mike? NOT ~~*Do you can see Mike?*~~

- You use the base form of the verb (not the infinitive) after *do, does,* or *did* in a question.
  Do you come here often? NOT ~~*Do you to come here often?*~~
  Did Helen enjoy the play? NOT ~~*Did Helen to enjoy the play?*~~
  NOT ~~*Did Helen enjoyed the play?*~~

- When a question word, e.g. *who, what, where, why, how,* etc. is the subject of a question, you put it before the verb. You don't use *do, does* or *did.*
  Who said that? NOT ~~*Who did say that?*~~
  What happened last night? NOT ~~*What did happen last night?*~~

- When a question word, e.g. *who, what, where, why, how,* etc. is the object of a question, you use normal question word order with *do, does* or *did.*
  Where do you live? *What car does he drive?* *Why did you go?*

Question tags

Test it ✓

1 Choose the best option.

- **a** You can't use spreadsheets, can you/can't you?
- **b** I'm right again, aren't I/amn't I?
- **c** They haven't got a car, haven't they/have they?
- **d** It's very cold today, isn't it/is it?
- **e** He forgot to post the letter, hasn't he/didn't he?
- **f** Sarah won't come, will Sarah/will she?
- **g** The weather was terrible, wasn't it/was it?
- **h** John's got brown eyes, has he/hasn't he?
- **i** I look silly in this jumper, aren't I/don't I?
- **j** You'd like to watch the film, wouldn't you/would you?

2 Choose the best option, A or B.

- **a** I'm not stupid, ... ?
  A am I **B** aren't I
- **b** They live in Japan, ... ?
  A live they **B** don't they
- **c** We can go by car, ... ?
  A can't we **B** can we
- **d** She eats meat, ... ?
  A isn't she **B** doesn't she
- **e** We can't leave yet, ... ?
  A can we **B** can't we
- **f** You won't tell anyone, ... ?
  A will you **B** are you
- **g** They'll come to the party, ... ?
  A won't they **B** can't they
- **h** You can't come tomorrow, ... ?
  A do you **B** can you
- **i** I'm wrong, ... ?
  A aren't I **B** amn't I
- **j** Beethoven was German, ... ?
  A wasn't he **B** was he?

| | 20 |

GO to page 80 and check your answers.

Test it again ✓

1 Write the correct question tag for each of these statements.

a You haven't eaten all the cake, ... ?

b Cats can swim, ... ?

c Leo doesn't know Martin, ... ?

d I'm going to be late, ... ?

e Shirley won't mind, ... ?

f You bought some milk, ... ?

g The meal last night was delicious, ... ?

h John didn't read the email, ... ?

i It's going to rain, ... ?

j She's got the keys, ... ?

2 Write the correct question tags in the dialogue.

Nick: You went to the match yesterday, [a].. ?

Jim: No, I missed it. But they're showing it on Channel 5 tonight, [b].. ?

Nick: Yes. You couldn't record it for me, [c].. ?

Jim: Yes, sure. Oh that's right! You've got to work tonight, [d].. ?

Nick: Unfortunately, yes. I'm a bit stupid really, [e].. ?

Jim: No. Why? You didn't volunteer to work tonight, [f].. ?

Nick: Yes, I did. The boss needed some extra help.

Jim: Oh dear. Sarah's going to be furious, [g].. ?

Nick: Why? I haven't forgotten something, [h].. ?

Jim: Well, it's your anniversary today, [i].. ?

Oh no, Nick! You haven't bought her a present, [j].. ?

☐ 20

Fix it

Answers to Test it

Check your answers. Wrong answer? Read the right Fix it note to find out why.

1
- **a** can you? → B
- **b** aren't I? → E
- **c** have they? → B
- **d** isn't it? → A
- **e** didn't he? → D
- **f** will she? → C
- **g** wasn't it? → A
- **h** hasn't he? → A
- **i** don't I? → D
- **j** wouldn't you? → A

2
- **a** A → B
- **b** B → D
- **c** A → A
- **d** B → D
- **e** A → B
- **f** A → C
- **g** A → C
- **h** B → C
- **i** A → E
- **j** A → A

Now go to page 79. Test yourself again.

Answers to Test it again

1
- **a** have you?
- **b** can't they?
- **c** does he?
- **d** aren't I?
- **e** will she?
- **f** didn't you?
- **g** wasn't it?
- **h** did he?
- **i** isn't it?
- **j** hasn't she?

2
- **a** didn't you?
- **b** aren't they?
- **c** could you?
- **d** haven't you?
- **e** aren't I?
- **f** did you?
- **g** isn't she?
- **h** have I?
- **i** isn't it?
- **j** have you?

Fix it notes

A

Use a negative question tag if the statement is positive.

B

Use a positive question tag if the statement is negative.

C

Make question tags with auxiliary verb + pronoun or *be* + pronoun, depending on what's used in the statement.

D

If there isn't an auxiliary verb or *be* in the statement, use the correct form of *do* in the question tag.

E

The negative question tag for *I am/I'm* is *aren't I?*

For more information, see the Review page opposite.

Question tags

- Question tags are extremely common in spoken English. They're used for two reasons: one is to ask a real question when you're not sure what the answer is; the other is to ask for someone's agreement or to check that they think the same as you do.
  Jane's a vegetarian, isn't she? (Real question. I'm not 100% sure of the answer.)
  It's really cold today, isn't it? (I expect you to agree with me.)

- There are three ways of making question tags.
  1 Auxiliary verb, e.g. *can, have, will*, etc., + pronoun
  You can drive, can't you? NOT ~~*You can drive, don't you?*~~
  (*Can* in the statement and in the question tag.)
  2 The verb *be* + pronoun
  He's French, isn't he? NOT ~~*He's French, hasn't he?*~~
  (*Be* in the statement and in the question tag.)
  3 A form of *do* + pronoun
  Cathy eats fish, doesn't she? NOT ~~*Cathy eats fish, isn't she?*~~
  (Ordinary verb in the statement, *do* in the question tag.)

- You use a pronoun in a question tag, not someone's name.
  Jill's coming tonight, isn't she? NOT ~~*Jill's coming tonight, isn't Jill?*~~

- You use a negative question tag if the statement is positive.
  I'm silly, aren't I? *You've got a car, haven't you?*
  They can do it, can't they? *She'll come, won't she?*
  He likes fish, doesn't he?

  Note: The negative question tag for *I am* is *aren't I?* (NOT ~~*amn't I?*~~).
  I'm coming with you, aren't I? *I'm a bit silly sometimes, aren't I?*

- You use a positive question tag if the statement is negative.
  I wasn't listening, was I? *It can't possibly work, can it?*
  We haven't got any milk, have we? *You won't tell her, will you?*
  They didn't ring, did they?

Short answers

Test it ✓

1 Choose the best option, A or B.

a Do you drive a Citroën?
A Yes, I don't. **B** No, I don't.
b Have you finished the report?
A No, I haven't. **B** No, I didn't.
c Is Katy going out tonight?
A No, Katy isn't. **B** No, she isn't.
d No one listens to a word I say.
A No, they do! **B** Yes, they do!
e Do you live in a city?
A Yes, I live in a city. **B** Yes, I do.
f Who's coming to dinner?
A Guy and Ann are coming to dinner. **B** Guy and Ann are.
g Is Neil taking his driving test next week?
A Yes, he is. **B** Yes, he's.
h Which horse won the race?
A The white horse did. **B** The white horse won the race.
i Is Elizabeth a teacher?
A Yes, Elizabeth is a teacher. **B** Yes, she is.
j Everyone laughs at Jonathan.
A No, they don't. **B** No, they do.

2 Choose the best option.

a Who wants more coffee? Patrick does/Patrick wants.
b Are you going to the office? No, I'm not/I don't.
c Can you help me? Yes, I am/I can.
d Does Isabelle live in Brussels? No, she doesn't/she isn't.
e Who broke the window? We did/We broke.
f Hasn't this computer got speakers? No, it hasn't/it has.
g No one likes me! Yes, they do/they like.
h Will it be warm in the Canaries? Yes, it will/it is.
i Is Jean-Luc Swiss? No, he isn't/Jean-Luc isn't.
j Are you happy? Yes, I am/I'm.

☐ 20

GO to page 84 and check your answers.

Test it again ✔

1 Match the questions to the answers.

a	Do you like tea, Sarah?	**1**	No, they didn't.
b	Would you marry Simon?	**2**	Yes, I can.
c	Who's on the phone?	**3**	Yes, I did.
d	Haven't you been to India?	**4**	No, I don't.
e	Will Karl come for lunch?	**5**	She did.
f	Can you swim?	**6**	Yes, we do.
g	Do you sell stamps?	**7**	Nick is.
h	Did you see the film last night?	**8**	Yes, he will.
i	Who said that?	**9**	No, I haven't.
j	Did they visit Sri Lanka?	**10**	No, I wouldn't.

2 Find and correct the mistakes in the short answers.

a What are those?
It's insects.

b Who's at the door?
Fred is.

c Haven't you done it yet?
No, he hasn't.

d Is it going to snow?
Yes, it can.

e Do you like it?
Yes, I like.

f Paul's a yoga teacher, isn't he?
Yes, he is.

g No one believes her.
No, they do!

h Who told you that?
Johnny told me that.

i Will you always love me?
Yes, I will.

j Do I need a passport?
No, you don't need.

☐ 20

Fix it

Answers to Test it

Check your answers. Wrong answer? Read the right Fix it note to find out why.

1
- **a** B → E
- **b** A → A
- **c** B → B
- **d** B → E
- **e** B → C
- **f** B → D
- **g** A → A
- **h** A → D
- **i** B → C
- **j** A → E

2
- **a** Patrick does. → D
- **b** I'm not. → A
- **c** I can. → A
- **d** she doesn't. → A
- **e** We did. → D
- **f** it hasn't. → E
- **g** they do. → F
- **h** it will. → A
- **i** he isn't. → B
- **j** I am. → A

Now go to page 83. Test yourself again.

Answers to Test it again

1
- **a** 4
- **b** 10
- **c** 7
- **d** 9
- **e** 8
- **f** 2
- **g** 6
- **h** 3
- **i** 5
- **j** 1

2
- **a** ~~It's~~ They're
- **b** correct
- **c** ~~he hasn't.~~ I/We haven't.
- **d** ~~it can.~~ it is.
- **e** ~~I like.~~ I do.
- **f** correct
- **g** ~~No, they do!~~ Yes, they do./No, they don't.
- **h** ~~told me that?~~ did.
- **i** correct
- **j** ~~you don't need.~~ you don't.

Fix it notes

A
Use the same auxiliary in a short answer as the auxiliary in the question. Don't contract the auxiliary in a positive short answer.

B
Use a suitable pronoun in short answers. Don't repeat the noun from the question.

C
Don't repeat all the words in a question when you give an answer unless there's a very good reason to.

D
If the subject of a question is a question word, e.g. *which*, *who*, etc, use subject + auxiliary in the short answer.

E
If the short answer starts with *Yes*, use a positive auxiliary or form of *do*. If the short answer starts with *No*, use a negative auxiliary or form of *do*.

F
If the short answer comes after a statement without an auxiliary verb, use the correct form of *do* (not the main verb in the statement) in the short answer.

For more information, see the Review page opposite.

Short answers

It's natural to use short answers to reply to questions. A short answer to a *yes/no* question can sound more polite or stronger than just 'Yes' or 'No'.

- You use the same auxiliary in a short answer as the auxiliary in the question.
  'Have you got a pen?' 'Yes, I have.' *'Will he go?' 'Yes, he will.'*
  'Would it matter?' 'No, it wouldn't.' *'Can you help me?' 'No, I can't.'*

  Note: You don't contract auxiliaries in positive short answers.
  Yes, I am. NOT ~~*Yes, I'm.*~~ *Yes, you have.* NOT ~~*Yes, you've.*~~
  Yes, they will. NOT ~~*Yes, they'll.*~~

- You use a suitable pronoun in short answers. You don't repeat the noun.
  'Are you coming?' 'No, I'm not.'
  'Is Peter Irish?' 'Yes, he is.' NOT ~~*'Yes, Peter is.'*~~

- You don't usually repeat all the words in a question when you give an answer unless there's a very good reason to.
  'Who's playing in the match?' 'Oscar and Fred are'.
  NOT ~~*'Oscar and Fred are playing in the match.'*~~

- You can repeat all the words in the question if you want to give your answer extra strength. This is common when you're disagreeing with someone.
  'You didn't tell the truth, did you?' 'Yes, I did tell the truth!'

- If the subject of a question is a question word, e.g. *who, which*, you use subject + auxiliary for the short answer.
  'Who said that?' 'I did.' *'Which suits me best?' 'The red one does.'*

- If the short answer starts with *Yes*, you use a positive auxiliary or form of *do*. If the short answer starts with *No*, you use a negative auxiliary or form of *do*.
  Yes, I can. *Yes, we have.* *Yes, they do.*
  No, you won't. *No, they can't.* *No, they don't.*

  You can also use a short answer to agree or disagree with what someone says. You use the same auxiliary in the short answer as in the statement.
  'Lisa's married to Jake.' 'No, she isn't.'

- If there isn't an auxiliary in the statement, use the correct form of *do*. Don't use the main verb from the statement in the short answer.
  'Tigers live in Africa.' 'No, they don't!' NOT ~~*'No, they don't live!'*~~

Useful grammar terms

Articles

There are two kinds of article: definite and indefinite. Articles go before a noun or an adjective + noun.

The is a definite article.
The house is in Sheep Street. *The black dog is mine.*

A and *an* are indefinite articles.
That's a camel. *Do you want an orange?* *I'm reading a good book.*

(See pages 9, 13 and 17.)

Adjectives

Adjectives tell you more about nouns. Adjectives can go before a noun or after the verb *be*.
Nick is a man. ➔ *Nick is an **intelligent** man.*
*Nick is **intelligent**.*

There are also comparative adjectives, e.g. *bigger, easier, more interesting,* and superlative adjectives, e.g. *biggest, easiest* and *the most interesting.*

(See pages 21, 25 and 33.)

Adverbs

Adverbs tell you more about verbs. They can describe the following things:

- how often something happens (adverbs of frequency), e.g. *never, rarely, occasionally, sometimes, often, usually, always, still,* etc.
- how certain something is (adverbs of certainty), e.g. *possibly, certainly, definitely,* etc.
- how you do an action (adverbs of manner), e.g. *carefully, slowly, fast,* etc.
- when something happens (adverbs of time), e.g. *yesterday, today, tomorrow,* etc.
- where something happens (adverbs of place), e.g. *here, there,* etc.

(See pages 21, 29 and 37.)

Nouns

Nouns are words you use to talk about people, animals, things, places and ideas.
Patrick is my brother. *I've got a dog.* *What's that box for?*
We live in a village. *Everybody needs love.*

Nouns can be the subject or object of a sentence.
My dog bit the postman. (The subject, *my dog,* is a noun. The object, *the postman,* is also a noun.)

Nouns are either countable, e.g. *apple, house,* etc., or uncountable, e.g. *advice, information, bread,* etc. Most common nouns are countable. You need to learn the uncountable ones. Many uncountable nouns in English are countable in other languages, so be careful!

(See pages 45 and 49.)

Pronouns

Pronouns replace nouns.

Subject pronouns are: *I, you, he, she, it, we, they.*
Helen is a patient person. ➔ *She's a patient person.*

Object pronouns are: *me, you, him, her, it, us, you them.*
Children like bananas. ➔ *Children like them.*

Possessive pronouns are: *my, your, his, her, its, our, their.*
That's Lisse's house. ➔ *That's her house.*

(See page 65.)

Quantifiers

Quantifiers are words that tell you about amounts. These are the most common quantifiers: *a, an, some, any, a lot, a bit, a few.*
I like you a lot. *There isn't any milk.* *How much cash have you got?*

(See page 53.)

Prepositions

There are prepositions and expressions of place, time and movement.
They do three things:

- *in, on, at, behind, under, on top of, at the bottom of,* etc. tell you where something is.
  The cat's behind the sofa. *The office is at the end of the street.*
- *in, on, at, tomorrow, last week,* etc. tell you when something happens.
  My birthday's in June. *We're sailing to France tomorrow.*
- *over, across, through,* etc. tell you how something moves and where it moves to.
  Tony ran across the road. *We drove over the bridge.*

(See pages 69 and 73.)

Question words

The most common question words are: *who, what, which, where, when, why, how, whose.* You can use question words to ask about people, things, places, time, reasons, and possessions.
Who's that? *What colour is the sky?* *Where have you been?*
When are they leaving? *Why are you laughing?* *How did he do that?*
Whose book is this?

A question word can be the subject or object of a sentence.
'Who saw you?' 'Mike saw me.' (*Who* is the subject.)
'Who did you see?' 'I saw David.' (*Who* is the object.)

(See pages 77, 81 and 85.)